African Proverbs
and Wisdom

Other Books by Julia Stewart

1,001 African Names (Citadel Press, 1996)
The African-American Books of Days (Citadel Press, 1996)
African Names (Citadel Press, 1993)

African Proverbs and Wisdom

▼▲▼▲▼▲▼▲▼▲▼

A Collection for Every Day of the Year
From More Than Forty African Nations

JULIA STEWART

Illustrations by Todd H. Schaffer

A CITADEL PRESS BOOK
Published by Carol Publishing Group

A Citadel Press Book
Published by Carol Publishing Group
Citadel Press is a registered trademark of Carol Communications, Inc.

Editorial, sales and distribution, rights and permissions inquiries should be
addressed to Carol Publishing Group, 120 Enterprise Avenue, Secaucus, N.J.
07094

In Canada: Canadian Manda Group, One Atlantic Avenue, Suite 105, Toronto,
Ontario M6K 3E7

Carol Publishing Group books may be purchased in bulk at special discounts
for sales promotion, fund-raising, or educational purposes. Special editions
can be created to specifications. For details, contact Special Sales Department,
120 Enterprise Avenue, Secaucus, N.J. 07094.

Manufactured in the United States of America

10 9 8 7 6 5 4 3 2 1

Library of Congress Cataloging-in-Publication Data

Stewart, Julia.
    African proverbs and wisdom : a collection for every day of the
year from more than forty African nations / Julia Stewart; illustrated
by Todd Schaffer.
        p.   cm.
    "A Citadel Press book."
    ISBN 0-8065-1807-3
    1. Proverbs, African.   I. Title.
PN6519.A6S74   1997
398.9'096—dc20   96-27995
                                                       CIP

This one is for Amanda, Jessica, and Megan

Introduction

The darkest thing about Africa has always been our ignorance of it.

George Kimble, *Reporter,* May 15, 1951

Over many centuries African peoples have produced an abundance of proverbs, legends, fables, riddles, superstitions, songs, poetry, stories, and quotes. Only a fraction of this creative treasure has been captured in print, thereby making it available to the wider world. Much of it remains unrecorded as it continues to be passed down orally from generation to generation. Because of the oral nature of African wisdom, parts of it disappear in the wind with each passing generation. "When an elder dies," recognizes one African proverb, "it is as if a whole library had burned down."

It has been said there are "as many books about Africa as there are Africans." Yet, suprisingly, a limited number of books are available that have been written *by* Africans, especially considering that there are over fifty African countries and that people have inhabited the continent since the dawn of human existence.

Why is this? Of the hundreds of indigenous African languages and dialects, few were committed to the written world until this century. Ge'ez (an ancient script of Ethiopia), the Vai language of Liberia, and Tamachek (a Berber dialect) are exceptions. The language of the Somalis—those celebrated bards of the desolate Horn of Africa—was not officially written until 1972.

During the colonial era, from the late 1800s through the 1960s, Europeans dominated large swaths of the African continent and promoted their languages at the expense of indigenous tongues. As we approach the twenty-first century, local markets for literature continue to be restricted by high illiteracy rates, low incomes, and multilingual societies. This makes the prospect of nurturing writers nothing less than a labor of love. By no means is this meant as a condemnation of Africa's literary scene. Quite the contrary. African literature that has been produced tends to be powerful, meaningful, and insightful. What a marvelous day it will be when there are as many books *by* Africans as there are Africans; conceivably each one would have a story to tell.

Author's Notes

Some genres of African literature are more plentiful than others. Proverbs, for instance, can be found by the thousands and many of them are included in this book. Despite their abundance, it requires some sifting to find proverbs that are pithy and at the same time easily translatable. For example, the proverb "A child acquires habits while still in the *ngozi* (a cloth for carrying children on the back of the mother)" requires explanation and doesn't relate to our way of child rearing.

Many African cultures assign great importance to proverbs. The ability to use proverbs effectively in speech and conversation is essential to attaining positions of leadership and respect in some African societies. Several proverbs themselves attest to the importance of this trait. "One who applies proverbs gets what he wants," suggests a Shona of Zimbabwe proverb. "A wise man who knows proverbs reconciles difficulties," claim the Yoruba of Nigeria. And in Sierra Leone it is said that "Proverbs are the daughters of experience."

African holidays and celebrations are indicated on the day on which they occur. Most of these dates were found in the *Europa World Year Book 1995*. Additional efforts were made to verify holidays with the embassies of the countries concerned. Should readers be interested in more information on a specific holiday, they might begin by contacting the country's embassy or tourism board, or by consulting country guidebooks. National holidays and observances are reported as given by embassies or reference sources. Their inclusion in this book indicates neither the author's nor the publisher's endorsement of governments' policies.

Muslim holidays are celebrated throughout Africa wherever Muslim populations are found; likewise with Christian holidays. The major Muslim and Christian observations are listed in the body of this book. However, they are not listed separately under each country in the "Holidays by Country Index." The Islamic calendar is based on lunar months; therefore, the dates of Muslim holidays change every year, falling about eleven days earlier each year. Dates given are approximations. Readers interested in more details on religious holidays can start by consulting *Religious Holidays and Calendars* by Aidan Kelly and others. (1993).

African Proverbs and Wisdom

▼▲▼▲▼▲▼▲▼▲▼▲▼

January 1

Life has a way of catching you unaware. Suddenly a year has gone by or many years and you hadn't noticed it. Suddenly you realize that your hair has grown white and you hadn't noticed it. Or that another life is being planned; unseen activities which touch upon your life, but go unperceived. And suddenly someone is getting married and it is your little sister, and you are watching her look into the future with large, round, sparkling eyes; you were too busy with the mechanics of life to notice the movements of her heart, the undulations of her soul, and the explosion of her happiness.

> Laila Said, Egyptian playwright, director, and teacher. From *A Bridge Through Time: A Memoir*, 1985.

New Year's Day, celebrated throughout Africa
Independence Day, Sudan

▼▲▼▲▼▲▼▲▼▲▼▲▼

January 2

Kanuri of West Africa riddle:
What is it that even the ostrich with its long neck and sharp eyes cannot see?

Answer: What will happen tomorrow.

New Year's Day (observed both January 1 and January 2), Mauritius

▼▲▼▲▼▲▼▲▼▲▼▲▼

January 3

Beyond the refusal of all exterior domination is the urge to reconnect in a deep way with Africa's cultural heritage, which has been far too long misunderstood and rejected. Far from being a superficial or folkloric attempt to bring back to life some of the traditions or practices of our ancestors, it is a matter of constructing a new African society, whose identity is not confused from outside.

> Paul Zoungrana, religious leader from Upper Volta (now
> Burkina Faso)

Revolution Day (anniversary of the 1966 coup), Burkina Faso

▼▲▼▲▼▲▼▲▼▲▼▲▼

January 4

It is easy enough to shout slogans, to sign manifestos, but it is quite a different matter to build, manage, command, spend days and nights seeking the solution to problems.

> Patrice Lumumba, nationalist leader of the Belgian Congo
> (now Zaire)

Day of the Martyrs of Independence, Zaire

▼▲▼▲▼▲▼▲▼▲▼▲▼

January 5

Beauty is half a God-given favor; intelligence a whole one.

> Fulani of West Africa proverb

Top of gold staff from West Africa

▼▲▼▲▼▲▼▲▼▲▼▲▼

January 6

THE CLEVER BRIDE
A Riddle From Eritrea

There once was a clever bride who lived with her mother-in-law and was very fond of chickpeas. The bride liked them so much that she would steal some from the kitchen every day to roast and eat in secret. Before long, half the sack of chickpeas was gone and the mother-in-law was very angry. She suspected the bride and mumbled to herself, "I'm certain she's a thief. She's the only new person in the house.

The mother-in-law was smart, but the bride was even more clever. She knew she was being suspected. One day, while cleaning with her mother-in-law, the young bride found a chickpea on the floor. She picked it up, showed it to her mother-in-law, and said three words that convinced the older woman that she hadn't been the thief.

What did the bride say?

Answer: "What is this?" The mother-in-law could not accuse the bride of stealing something that she had never seen before.

▼▲▼▲▼▲▼▲▼▲▼▲▼

January 7

Ethiopian superstition says that if you don't laugh during Christmas you won't be happy for the rest of your life.

Coptic Christmas, Egypt, Eritrea, Ethiopia, Sudan
Pioneer's Day, Liberia

Cross pendant depicting Mary from Ethiopia

▼▲▼▲▼▲▼▲▼▲▼▲▼

January 8

WHY DOGS SNIFF AT ONE ANOTHER'S TAILS
A South African Fable

Listen and I will tell you why dogs sniff each other's tails every time they meet. There was a time—long, long ago—when dogs were free from the service of man. O child of man, look into the dog's face and you will see he is sad, for he pines for his freedom and for the days when he ruled his own kingdom, and how these things were lost.

It happened this way. A quarrel arose between the kingdom of man and the kingdom of the dog, and a mighty war was waged.

The army of man proved to be too strong for the dog, and man won the war. Because man is great and wise and just, he sent a letter to make peace with his enemy. In the letter man wrote, "Your liberty will be granted if you will accept our terms."

The dogs rejoiced at this news and penned a reply, which said, "O wise man, O great man, we accept your terms, and we thank you for the generous offer of peace." They tied this letter to the tail of the most trusted dog and dispatched the messenger to the kingdom of man.

Alas, the messenger strayed, and man never did receive the acceptance of peace. Thus the dog became the servant of man. But the dog has never given up hope. Do you not see him wandering in strange places, looking for stray dogs? When he sees one, he will joyfully run to greet him and sniff around the tail, relentlessly searching for the letter lost so long ago. For the dog is sure that someday the letter will be found and he shall once again be free from the service of man.

▼▲▼▲▼▲▼▲▼▲▼▲▼

January 9

The one-eyed man doesn't thank God until he sees a blind man.

Fulani of West Africa proverb

▼▲▼▲▼▲▼▲▼▲▼▲▼

January 10

It is man who counts.
I call upon gold:
It answers not.
I call upon rich fabric:
It answers not.
It is man who counts.

Traditional Akan of Ghana poem

▼▲▼▲▼▲▼▲▼▲▼▲▼

January 11

It is not rushing that is important, it is making sure.

Maasai of East Africa proverb

▼▲▼▲▼▲▼▲▼▲▼▲▼

January 12

When the flute is played in Zanzibar, all Africa east of the Lakes must dance.

Arab proverb recalling the infuence the island of Zanzibar once had over the East African region

What there is in Pemba there is in Zanzibar as well.

Swahili proverb

Zanzibar Revolution Day, Tanzania

▼▲▼▲▼▲▼▲▼▲▼▲▼

January 13

Don't look for speed in a cheap horse; be content if it neighs.

Hausa of West Africa proverb

Liberation Day (anniversary of the 1967 coup), Togo

▼▲▼▲▼▲▼▲▼▲▼▲▼

January 14

In the time of happiness:

> Ships ply the river;
> They move north and south.
> Men build temples and dig ponds;
> They make plantations of trees for the gods.

In the time of happiness:

> The people make merry:
> They drink in the gladness of their hearts.
> For a man can put his bed in the shade,
> And sleep safely behind his own gate.

Ipuwer, ancient Egyptian prophet. From the "Admonitions of a Prophet," written around the end of the Sixth Dynasty (2420–2258 B.C.)

▼▲▼▲▼▲▼▲▼▲▼▲▼

January 15

More adhesive than a tick.

Egyptian expression for a clingy person

▼▲▼▲▼▲▼▲▼▲▼▲▼

January 16

Palibe munthu anasula mfuti nkhondo itafika m'mudzi mwace.

A person does not begin to forge a gun when the war has already arrived in the village.

Nyanja of Malawi proverb on preparedness

John Chilembwe Day (commemorates the freedom fighter's struggle against British colonial rule), Malawi

▼▲▼▲▼▲▼▲▼▲▼▲▼

January 17

Pendo Halijui Siri

Love Does Not Know Secrets

Pendo halijui siri
likifichwa hufichuka.

Love knows no secrets,
when it is hidden it will be
   discovered.

Pendo halina hiyari
mtu linapomshika
kulla jambo atakiri
jambo lisilofanyika.

Love has no choice;
when it seizes a man,
he will confess everything,
everything that was not done.

Pendo halina huruma
kizee hufedheheka

Love has no pity,
even an old man may be put to
   shame,

pendo halirudi nyuma
kwa kitu linachotaka.
Mtu likimuandama
majununi hugeuka.

love does not return
to a thing it desires.
When it pursues a man,
he turns mad.

Pendo humdhili mtu
mwili wake hudhofika
akidhilika mwenzetu
haifai kumcheka
Pendo mtu hadhubutu
kando-kando kuliweka.

Love humbles a man,
his body becomes emaciated;
when a friend of ours is humiliated
it is not fair to laugh at him.
A man does not have the stamina
to put love aside.

Pendo katu haliridhi
kitu kiwe cha shirika.
Pendo unapoliudhi
mara moja kuyayuka.
Pendo huwa ni maradhi
mabaya yasotibika.

Love never agrees
to share with anything.
If you irritate love,
you melt away at once.
Love is a disease,
a malignant incurable disease.

Swahili love poem

▼▲▼▲▼▲▼▲▼▲▼▲▼

January 18

Hit him with a bean, he will break.

Tunisian expression describing a weak person

National Revolution Day, Tunisia

▼▲▼▲▼▲▼▲▼▲▼▲▼

January 19

Ethiopia is a land where the great unknown yonder still exists in plenty.

Slogan written on Ethiopian airlines tickets

...thirteen months of sunshine...

Slogan used by Ethiopian tourist posters. Refers to the Ethiopian calendar, which has thirteen months

Timket (Eastern Orthodox Epiphany), Ethiopia, Eritrea

▼▲▼▲▼▲▼▲▼▲▼▲▼

January 20

According to local legend of the Cape Verde Islands, located 385 miles (620 kilometers) off the west coast of Africa, when God had finished creating the heavens and the earth, he rubbed his hands together in satisfaction. Some crumbs fell from his hands and scattered unnoticed into the Atlantic Ocean, creating the Cape Verde islands. A similar legend is told in the Indian Ocean islands of Africa.

National Heroes' Day (anniversary of the death of Amílcar Cabral), Guinea-
Bissau, Cape Verde
Army Day, Mali

▼▲▼▲▼▲▼▲▼▲▼▲▼

January 21

Be it wickedness or be it goodness, neither goes unrequited.

Yoruba of Nigeria proverb

Mask from Nigeria

▼▲▼▲▼▲▼▲▼▲▼▲▼

January 22

To be impartial... is indeed to have taken sides already... with the status quo.

Archbishop Desmond Tutu of South Africa. From *Hope and Suffering*, 1984

▼▲▼▲▼▲▼▲▼▲▼▲▼

January 23

The tar of my country is better than the honey of other countries.

Moroccan proverb on patriotism

▼▲▼▲▼▲▼▲▼▲▼▲▼

January 24

The drunkenness of youth has passed like a fever,
  and yet I saw many things.
Seeing my glory in the days of my glory.
The feet of my warhorse
Drummed upon the cities of the world;
  I sacked great towns like a hot wind
And fell like thunder upon far lands.
The kings of the earth were dragged behind my chariot
  And the people of the earth behind my laws;
But now
The drunkenness of youth has passed like a fever,
  like foam upon sand.
Death took me in a net;
  My armies warred against him in vain.
  Listen, O wayfarer, to the words of my death,
For they were not the words of my life:

Save up your soul
And taste the beautiful wine of peace,
   For tomorrow the earth shall answer:
He is with me,
   My jealous beast holds him for ever.

Anonymous. Inscription at the city of Brass, Nigeria, c.
thirteenth century A.D.

Day of Victory (anniversary of failed attack at Sarakawa), Togo

▼▲▼▲▼▲▼▲▼▲▼▲▼▲▼

January 25

By trying repeatedly, the monkey learns to jump from the tree.

Cameroonian proverb on perseverance

Mount Cameroon Race: Guinness sponsors a twenty-seven-kilometer footrace
up and down Mount Cameroon, which takes place on the last Sunday of
January every year

Brass chameleon pendant of the Tikar of Cameroon

▼▲▼▲▼▲▼▲▼▲▼▲▼▲▼

January 26

Teach me to laugh once more
let me laugh with Africa my mother
I want to dance to her drum-beats

I am tired of her cries
scream with laughter
roar with laughter
Oh, how I hate this groaning.

Grace Akello, Ugandan poet. From "Encounter"

National Resistance Movement Anniversary Day, Uganda

▼▲▼▲▼▲▼▲▼▲▼▲▼▲▼

January 27

Laugh at the madman only when you have stopped bearing children.

Shona of Zimbabwe proverb warning against delighting in other people's misfortune because your turn may be next

▼▲▼▲▼▲▼▲▼▲▼▲▼▲▼

January 28

The future beckons at us to dare the monsters that menace us. We are no fools for entering the social struggle even though we perish, for wise men still believe that it is better to be maimed or killed in their affray than to live like a slave.

Mowugo Okoye, Nigerian writer

▼▲▼▲▼▲▼▲▼▲▼▲▼▲▼

January 29

Tradition has it that the poet on his horse stood between the massed opposing forces and, with a voice charged with drama and emotion, chanted the better part of the day until the men, smitten with force of his delivery, dropped their arms and embraced one another.

Said Sheikh Samatar, Somali scholar. Samatar describes the
traditional power of the poet in Somalia

▼▲▼▲▼▲▼▲▼▲▼▲▼

January 30

*Mtu akiinuka akaona nguo imemganda matakoni basi inaonyesha kuwa
mtu huyo ana tabia ya kusema uwongo.*

If a person stands up and his clothes stick between his buttocks it
means he is in the habit of telling lies.

Swahili of East Africa superstition

▼▲▼▲▼▲▼▲▼▲▼▲▼

January 31

Atigarite mwoo wa nguku.

He had a chicken's life left in him.

Embu of Kenya expression meaning that a person was very
close to death

▼▲▼▲▼▲▼▲▼▲▼▲▼

February 1

One of the ways of helping to destroy a people is to tell them they don't have a history, that they have no roots.

> Archbishop Desmond Tutu of South Africa

A people denied history is a people deprived of dignity.

> Ali A. Mazrui, Kenyan scholar

The African people cannot be read out of history. Not to know what one's race has done in former times is to continue always as a child. The African himself expresses the thought in saying "knowing thyself better than he who speaks of thee. Not to know is bad; not to wish to know is worse."

> Julius K. Nyerere, first president of Tanzania

▼▲▼▲▼▲▼▲▼▲▼▲▼

February 2

However far the stream flows, it never forgets its source.

> Yoruba of Nigeria proverb

Bronze pendant of a pregnant woman of the Abron of Côte d'Ivoire

▼▲▼▲▼▲▼▲▼▲▼▲▼

February 3

On my visits to America, I discovered that old Marxist dictum, "From each according to his abilities, to each according to his needs," was probably more in force in America—that holy of holies of capitalism—than in any other country in the world.

Félix Houphouët-Boigny, first president of Côte d'Ivoire

Heroes' Day (anniversary of the the assassination of Eduardo Mondlane), Mozambique

▼▲▼▲▼▲▼▲▼▲▼▲▼

February 4

The day we came we ate off dishes, now we are eating out of wooden bowls.

Ovimbundu of Angola proverb on wearing out one's welcome

Commencement of the Armed Struggle (against Portuguese colonialism), Angola
Thaipoosam Cavadee (Tamil religious observance), Mauritius

▼▲▼▲▼▲▼▲▼▲▼▲▼

February 5

It is always right for one to strike for one's own liberty. Blacks must look around themselves, and not afar, for the instruments and forces that must be utilized for their salvation. Neither institution nor friends can make a race stand unless it has strength in its own legs. Races, like individuals, must stand or fall by their own merits. It is only through struggle and the surmounting of difficulties that races, like individuals, are made strong, powerful and useful. This is the road that the black man should travel; this is the road, I think, the black man will travel.

We are not only men linked to Africa by birth and history. We are also citizens of our own nations; we are also Christians, or Moslems, socialists, conservatives, or communists. These are more truly a reflection of ourselves than is our color or ancestry.

Julius K. Nyerere, first president of Tanzania

Youth Day, Tanzania

▼▲▼▲▼▲▼▲▼▲▼▲▼

February 6

We should go down to the grassroots of our culture, not to remain there, not to be isolated there, but to draw strength and substance therefrom, and with whatever additional resources of strength and material we acquire, proceed to set up a new form of society raised to the level of human progress.

Sékou Touré, first president of Guinea

▼▲▼▲▼▲▼▲▼▲▼▲▼

February 7

Nkosi sikele'iAfrica　　　　　God bless Africa
Maluphakanisw'uponso lwayo　Raise up her spirit
Yizwa imitandazo yetu　　　　Hear our prayers
Usi - sikelele　　　　　　　　And bless us

Sikelel'amadol'asizwe　　　　Bless the leaders
Sikelela kwa nomlisela　　　　Bless also the young
Ulitwal'ilizwe ngomonde　　　That they may carry the land
　　　　　　　　　　　　　　　　with patience
Uwusikilele　　　　　　　　　And that you may bless them

Sikelel'amalinga etu	Bless our efforts
Awonayana nokuzaka	To unite and lift ourselves up
Awemfundo nemvisiswano	Through learning and understanding
Uwasikelele	And bless them
Woza Moya! (Yihla) Moya!	Come Spirit! (Descend) Spirit!
Woza Moya Oyingcwele!	Come, Holy Spirit!

African national anthem

▼▲▼▲▼▲▼▲▼▲▼▲▼

February 8

Let us listen to the voices of our Forebears...
In the smoky cabin, souls that wish us well are murmuring.

Léopold Sédar Senghor, first president of Senegal. From "Nuit de Sine"

▼▲▼▲▼▲▼▲▼▲▼▲▼

February 9

THE TWO FIGHTERS
A Vai of Liberia Folktale

Once there was a burly man who loved to fight and who challenged everyone he met. He owned three cows, which he took with him as he traveled throughout the country, offering the animals to anyone who could defeat him. A lazy man heard about the fighter and sent word that he would accept the challenge. The lazy man gathered three of his own cows to wager against the champion. The fighter said, "Alright, we will fight tomorrow." Before the match, the lazy man informed his son that if the champion served him four good licks, he intended to run away. It wasn't long into the match before the strong man had delivered four hard punches. The lazy man cried out to his son, "I believe the time has come." The son replied, "Wait until he strikes you one more time." The champion thought to himself, "These people are going to wait until I punch the lazy man one more time and then they have something organized; surely they plan to kill me." He immediately stopped fighting and ran off without his cows. The lazy man was declared the winner and awarded all six cows.

The lesson: A fight is not always won by the strongest; sometimes it is won by he who holds out until the end.

▼▲▼▲▼▲▼▲▼▲▼▲▼

February 10

A good man will neither speak nor do as a bad man will; but if a man is bad, it makes no difference whether he be a black or a white devil.

> Ottobah Cogoano, *Thoughts and Sentiments of the Evils of Slavery*, 1787. Of Ghanaian origin, Cogoano became a prominent antislavery activist in England

▼▲▼▲▼▲▼▲▼▲▼▲▼

February 11

I have fought against white domination, and I have fought against black domination. I have cherished the idea of a democratic and free society in which all persons live together in harmony and with equal opportunities. It is an ideal which I hope to live for and to achieve. But if needs be, it is an ideal for which I am prepared to die.

> Nelson Mandela, president of South Africa. The closing statement of his speech delivered in Cape Town on February 11, 1990, the day he was released from prison after more than twenty-seven years. (This remark was originally made during the infamous Rivonia Trial of 1964, at which he was sentenced to life in prison)

Youth Day, Cameroon
Armed Forces Day, Liberia

▼▲▼▲▼▲▼▲▼▲▼▲▼

February 12

The king who governs [Ghana] at present... is called Tenkaminen;
Tenkaminen is the master of a large empire and a formidable
power.... The king of Ghana can put two hundred thousand
warriors in the field, more than forty thousand being armed with
bow and arrow.... When he gives audience to his people to listen
to their complaints and set them to rights, he sits in a pavilion
around which stand ten horses with gold-embroidered trappings.
Behind the king stand ten pages holding shields and gold-
mounted swords; on his right are the sons of princes of his empire,
splendidly clad and with gold plaited in their hair. The governor of
the city is seated on the ground in front of the king and all around
him are seated his viziers. The door of the pavilion is guarded by
dogs of an excellent breed who almost never leave the king's
presence and who wear collars of gold and silver, ornamented with
the same metals. The beginning of the royal audience is an-
nounced by the beating of a kind of drum which they call *deba*,
made of a long piece of hollowed wood. The people gather when
they hear this sound.

    Al Bekri, Moorish historian. From *Book of Roads and Kingdoms*,
A.D. 1067. Bekri describes the audiences of the King of Ghana

▼▲▼▲▼▲▼▲▼▲▼▲▼

February 13

Congolese riddle:
  Who can whistle from another man's mouth?

Answer: The other man.

▼▲▼▲▼▲▼▲▼▲▼▲▼▲▼

February 14

When I embrace her,
And her arms open wide,
I feel like a man in Spiceland,
Who is overwhelmed with perfume.

Then I kiss her;
And she opens her lips.
Without a taste of beer,
I am intoxicated.

Young man's love poem inscribed on a piece of broken pottery
from ancient Egypt. Written during the Nineteenth Dynasty, c.
1304–1085 B.C.

Love, you know, is strangely whimsical, containing affronts, jabs,
parleys, wars then peace again. Now, for you to ask advice to love
by, is as if you ask advice to run mad by.

Terence, a comic-poet of ancient Rome originally from
Carthage, North Africa (present-day Tunisia). From *The Eunuch*,
192–157 B.C.

▼▲▼▲▼▲▼▲▼▲▼▲▼▲▼

February 15

You know who you love;
you cannot know who loves you.

Yoruba of Nigeria proverb

Bronze head from Nigeria

▼▲▼▲▼▲▼▲▼▲▼▲▼

February 16

Plant shade trees around the edge of your pond,
And let your spirit rest under them.
Drink the water, and follow the desires of your heart.
Take hold of the opportunities of this world,
But give bread to the man without a field,
That you may assure yourself a good name for all
eternity.

Advice of Neferhotep, a high priest of Amon, ancient Egypt

▼▲▼▲▼▲▼▲▼▲▼▲▼

February 17

More rare than flea-brains.

Egyptian expression for scarce things

Maha Shivratree (Hindu festival), Mauritius

▼▲▼▲▼▲▼▲▼▲▼▲▼

February 18

There at the edge of town
Just by the burial ground
Stands the house without a shadow
Lived in by new skeletons.

That is all that is left
To greet us on the home coming
After we have paced the world.
And longed for returning.

Lenrie Peters, Gambian poet. "Home Coming"

Independence Day, Gambia

▼▲▼▲▼▲▼▲▼▲▼▲▼

February 19

In some ways Africa is a bewildering mosaic of cultures in a single continent. They used to call the United States a "melting pot" of different nationalities. On the whole, Africa is not a continent of immigrant peoples (though there are exceptions); it is more a continent of immigrant cultures.

Ali Mazrui, Kenya scholar. From "Africa's Triple Heritage and I," *Africa Events* magazine, July/August 1986

Chinese Spring Festival, Mauritius (date varies)

▼▲▼▲▼▲▼▲▼▲▼▲▼

February 20

A chief's son...should always keep a cool heart and remain patient. Rushing through things at a gallop, we risk burying someone alive; and a hasty tongue can ensnare us in troubles we cannot escape by flight.

Ahmadou Kourouma, Ivorian writer. From *The Suns of Independence*, 1968

▼▲▼▲▼▲▼▲▼▲▼▲▼

February 21

Africa my Africa
Africa of proud warriors or ancestral savannahs
Africa that my grandmother sings
On the bank of her distant river
I have never known you
But my face is full of your blood
Your beautiful black blood which water the wide fields

David Mandessi Diop, Senegalese poet. First stanza of "Africa," in *Coup de Pilons*, 1956

▼▲▼▲▼▲▼▲▼▲▼▲▼

February 22

When the time of the pilgrimage arrived, [the sultan of Egypt] sent [Mansa Musa] a large quantity of drachmas [silver coins], baggage camels, and choice riding camels with saddles and harness. [The sultan] caused abundant quantities of foodstuffs to be brought for his suite and followers, established posting-stations for the feeding of the animals and gave to the emirs of the pilgrimage a written order to look after and respect [the emperor of Mali]....

This man spread upon Cairo the flood of his generosity: there was no person, officer of the court or holder of any office of the sultanate who did not receive a sum in gold from him. The people of Cairo earned incalculable sums from him, whether by buying and selling or by gifts. So much gold was current in Cairo that it ruined the value of money.

> El Mehmendar, emir of Egypt. Mehmendar describes the
> stopover in Cairo made by Mansa Musa, emperor of Mali, in
> July 1324 during his famed pilgrimage to Mecca

Id-Ul-Fitr (end of Ramadan), observed in Muslim countries and communities across Africa (exact date depends upon sighting of the moon)

▼▲▼▲▼▲▼▲▼▲▼▲▼

February 23

Pang'ono - pang'ono kambe anafika ku Ciwambo.

Little by little, the tortoise arrived at the Indian Ocean.

Nyanja of Malawi proverb

▼▲▼▲▼▲▼▲▼▲▼▲▼

February 24

Through wisdom I have dived
down into the great sea,
and have seized in the place of her depths
a pearl whereby I am rich.
I went down like the great iron anchor,
whereby men anchor ships for the night
on the high seas,
and I received a lamp which lighteth me,
and I came up by the ropes
of the boat of understanding.

Queen of Sheba, Ethiopian queen, *Kebra Negast* (Glory of
Kings), a fourteenth-century chronicle of the Solomonic
dynasty

▼▲▼▲▼▲▼▲▼▲▼▲▼

February 25

Akitajwa mtu na pale pale akahudhuria, inaonyesha kuwa ataishi umri
mrefu; yaani atakufa mkongwe.

If a person who is being talked about appears in the middle of the
discussion, it means that he will live to a very old age.

Swahili of East Africa superstition

▼▲▼▲▼▲▼▲▼▲▼▲▼

• February 26

We are descended from india-rubber, and our great ancestor, if you
like, was Michelin, or rather the fellow you see on the posters
advertising that brand of tyres. That's why our forefathers and the
slaves who were sent to America were able to adapt themselves to a
situation that was new to them.

Sylvain Bemba, Congolese writer. From *The Dark Room*, 1964

▼▲▼▲▼▲▼▲▼▲▼▲▼

February 27

A man's deeds are of greater importance than the facts of his birth.

Maasai of East Africa proverb

▼▲▼▲▼▲▼▲▼▲▼▲▼

February 28

GOHA'S DEATH BED
An Egyptian Folktale

From his deathbed Goha called to his wife. He asked her to fix her long black hair neatly, apply her makeup generously, dress in her most elegant clothes, and come sit by his bedside. His distraught wife replied, "I can't think of such frivolous things while you are dying, and never will I again after you are gone. Goha demanded, "I am a dying man, do as I say." His wife complied. Sitting beside her husband in her finest gown, she asked, "Don't you want to gaze at my beauty before dying?" Goha replied, "No. They say 'Death chooses the best' and I hoped death might choose you instead of me."

Union Day, Egypt

▼▲▼▲▼▲▼▲▼▲▼▲▼

February 29
(leap year)

Go back and fetch what was left behind.

Akan of Ghana proverb

Catfish pendant of the Akan of Ghana

▼▲▼▲▼▲▼▲▼▲▼▲▼

March 1

The vigor and quality of a nation depend on its capacity to renew itself each generation.

Jomo Kenyatta, first president of Kenya, address to the Kenya Youth Festival, Nairobi, October 10, 1966

▼▲▼▲▼▲▼▲▼▲▼▲▼

March 2

Ethiopia has need of no one; she stretches out her hands to God

Menelik II, emperor of Ethiopia

Throughout history it has been the inaction of those who could have acted, the indifference of those who should have known better, the silence of the voice of justice when it mattered most, that has made it possible for evil to triumph.

Haile Selassie, emperor of Ethiopia. Opening statement to a special session of the UN General Assembly held in Addis Ababa on October 4, 1963

Victory of Adowa Day (commemorates victory of Menelik II over Italy in 1896), Ethiopia

▼▲▼▲▼▲▼▲▼▲▼▲▼

March 3

I have lived in the redness of the stones that mark a path through my blood; I am the descendant of a forgotten race, but I carry in my hands the remnants of their fire.

Mohammed Khair-Eddine, Moroccan writer and poet

My country is my country, even though it is unjust to me.

Moroccan proverb

Feast of the Throne (anniversary of King Hassan's ascension), Morocco
National Unity Day, Sudan
Martyr's Day, Malawi

▼▲▼▲▼▲▼▲▼▲▼▲▼

March 4

I see people looking like fire coming from where the sun sets. They have an iron rod. I don't know what sort of people they are. When you look at him, even [his] hair is like fire. And if he tries to shake his rod, all the people fall down. And that person, his war will not be resisted for he will be too strong. And he will come from where the sun sets.

When a highway is made through Kanyuambora, it will be used by an enemy whom none will understand in speech. An iron-mouthed animal will come and follow the highway.

Embu of Kenya elders quoting Mbogo wa Kirangi, a prophet
who predicted the coming of the white man

▼▲▼▲▼▲▼▲▼▲▼▲▼

March 5

Tamangira kuotha anasiya moto nueka.

Mr. Run-to-get-warm left the fire as it was beginning to blaze.

Nyanja of Malawi proverb

Independence Day, Equatorial Guinea

▼▲▼▲▼▲▼▲▼▲▼▲▼

March 6

One country, one people, one destiny.

Steadily and firmly we are building up a better and richer life for our people and our continent. The liberation flame, although feeble and glimmering, still grows brighter each day. And the time is approaching when a new civilization, a new culture, shall spring up from among our people, and the Nile shall once again flow through the land of science, of art and of literature, wherein will live Black Men of the highest accomplishments.

I can see springing up, cities of Africa becoming the metropolis of science and learning, architecture and philosophy. And the immortal are resounding the echo: *seek ye first the political kingdom and all things shall be added unto you.*

Kwame Nkrumah, first president of Ghana

Independence Day, Ghana

▼▲▼▲▼▲▼▲▼▲▼▲▼

March 7

Let us not run the world hastily;
Let us not grasp at the rope of wealth impatiently;
What should be treated with mature judgement
Let us not treat in a fit of temper

Yoruba of Nigeria maxims

▼▲▼▲▼▲▼▲▼▲▼▲▼

March 8

You may judge the strength of a nation by the political consciousness of its women.

Kwame Nkrumah, first president of Ghana

International Women's Day, observed by various countries
National Day, Libya

▼▲▼▲▼▲▼▲▼▲▼▲▼

March 9

By coming and going, a bird
weaves its nest.

Ashanti of Ghana proverb on
perseverance

Hornbill mask from Côte d'Ivoire

▼▲▼▲▼▲▼▲▼▲▼▲▼

March 10

Avoid a superior who is enraged,
Stay out of his path.
Answer him pleasantly, calm his wrath.
For the contentious man is beaten,
And rage destroys itself—it damages its own affairs.
One turns to praise you after his terrible hour
Because his heart received your soothing words.
Therefore, seek out silence and submission.

Advice from the "Wisdom of Ani," an ancient Egyptian
text believed to have been written by a scribe of the
house of Neferkareteri during the Eighteenth Dynasty
(1570–c. 1342 B.C.)

▼▲▼▲▼▲▼▲▼▲▼▲▼

March 11

The moment you have protected an individual, you have protected
society.

Kenneth Kaunda, first president of Zambia

Youth Day, Zambia
Commonwealth Day, Swaziland (date varies)

▼▲▼▲▼▲▼▲▼▲▼▲▼

March 12

The elephant never gets tired of carrying his tusks.

Vai of Liberia proverb on supportng your own people

Decoration Day, Liberia
National Day, Mauritius
Moshoeshoe Day (birthday of King Moshoeshoe I), Lesotho

▼▲▼▲▼▲▼▲▼▲▼▲▼

March 13

One should keep one's eyes on one's destination, not on where one stumbled.

Yoruba of Nigeria proverb

Festival mask from Nigeria

▼▲▼▲▼▲▼▲▼▲▼▲▼

March 14

THE TWO TRAVELERS
A Hausa of West Africa Folktale

There were two travelers who saw a bundle on the side of the road. Ali, who was walking in front, picked up the bundle and saw that there was money inside. Audu said, "What great fortune, we have come upon riches." Ali asked, "*We* have come upon riches, or *I* have come upon riches?" The two men entered a dark forest where some bandits approached them; the travelers ran away. After awhile, Ali became exhausted from the weight of the bundle and said, "Alas, I am too tired to carry it farther; today we will suffer loss." Adu asked, "*We* shall suffer loss, or *you* shall suffer loss?"

▼▲▼▲▼▲▼▲▼▲▼▲▼

March 15

One doesn't throw a stick after the snake has gone.

Liberian proverb

J. J. Robert's Birthday (commemorates the birthday of the first president), Liberia

▼▲▼▲▼▲▼▲▼▲▼▲▼

March 16

Tamu Ya Pendo Ni Nini?   **What Is The Sweetness of Love?**

Nawauliza suali   *I ask you a question*
enyi mnaopendana   *you who love one another,*
mnipe jibu la kweli   *give me a true answer,*
jawabu yenye maana: *a meaningful solution:*
pendo ni kitu thakili   *Love is a heavy thing,*
nahisi raha halina.   *I feel there is no joy in it.*

Tamu ya pendo ni nini   *What is the sweetness of love?*
nambieni waungwana   *Tell me, gentlefolk,*
nimefikiri yakini   *I have been thinking deeply,*
si usiku su mchana   *not by night alone, not by day alone;*
nimeshindwa kubaini   *I am at a loss to understand*
tamu yake kuiona.   *or to see its sweetness.*

Napenda toka zamani	*I have loved for a long time,*
si kama meanza jana	*it is not yesterday that I began,*
tamu yake siioni	*but I do not see the sweetness of it;*
illa adha kubwa sana	*nothing except a great deal of vexation,*
na adhabu ya moyoni	*and torment of the heart,*
kufanya si mtu tena.	*I am no longer capable of it.*
Nambieni waungwana	*Tell me, gentle folk,*
wawili mnaopendana	*who love one another in pairs,*
kweli raha mimi sina	*indeed I am without peace,*
pendo lanikera sana.	*love upsets me a great deal.*
Na kama tamu halina	*And if there is not sweetness in it,*
katu sitopenda tena.	*I will never love again.*

Swahili love poem

▼▲▼▲▼▲▼▲▼▲▼▲▼

March 17

It's better to be lucky than to be good.

Luo of Kenya proverb

▼▲▼▲▼▲▼▲▼▲▼▲▼

March 18

You will find no other lands, you will find no other sea.
The city will follow you.
You will roam the same streets,
grow old in the same quarters,
and turn grey amongst these same houses.
Always you will arrive in this city, Don't hope for any other.
There is no ship to take you away, no road out of town.
As you have destroyed your life here
In this small corner, you have ruined it throughout the world.

C. P. Cavafy, Egyptian poet. From "The City," 1910, trans. Paul
Strathern, in *The Complete Poems,* 1961

▼▲▼▲▼▲▼▲▼▲▼▲▼

March 19

M'kapeza eni akazinga maso, iwe mlendo ukazingenso lako.

If you should find the residents of a place frying their eyes, fry yours also.

> Nyanja of Malawi proverb equivalent to "When in Rome, do as
> the Romans do"

▼▲▼▲▼▲▼▲▼▲▼▲▼

March 20

The oriental girl will go to the West; and the Western girl will go to the Orient.

> Tunisian expression showing that one's destiny is unknown

Independence Day, Tunisia
Ougadi (Telegu festival), Mauritius

▼▲▼▲▼▲▼▲▼▲▼▲▼

March 21

●

It is fear that sets the racial moods, and if we are to break the vicious circle we must concentrate our assault upon these racial fears in all their forms. Hatred and intolerance are not innate in peoples; they are the children of fear, as fear is the child of ignorance.

> Robert Kweku Atta Gardiner, Ghanaian diplomat

The first step...is to make the black man come to himself; to pump back life into his empty shell; to infuse him wth pride and dignity, to remind him of his complicity in the crime of allowing himself to be misused and therefore letting evil reign supreme in the country of his birth.

> Steven Biko, South African political activist. From *I Write What I Like*, 1978

International Day for the Elimination of Racial Discrimination
  (United Nations observation in memory of victims of racial discrimination, prompted by police shootings of demonstrators in Sharpeville, South Africa, on March 21, 1960)
Human Rights Day, South Africa
Independence Day, Namibia
Youth Day, Tunisia
Mother's Day, Egypt
National Tree Planting Day, Lesotho

▼▲▼▲▼▲▼▲▼▲▼▲▼

March 22

Rather hear the flatulencies of camels than the prayers of the fishes.

> Egyptian expression used by those who prefer to travel by land rather than by sea

He who does not travel will not know the value of men.

> Moroccan proverb

▼▲▼▲▼▲▼▲▼▲▼▲▼

March 23

"Long long ago...God lived on earth or at least was very near to us. But there was a certain old woman who used to pound her fufu [cassava meal], and the pestle used to knock up against God. So God said to the old woman, 'Why do you always do that to me? Because of what you are doing I am going to take myself away up into the sky.' And of truth he did so."

> Akan of Ghana legend, as recorded by Basil Davidson in *The African Genius*, 1969

▼▲▼▲▼▲▼▲▼▲▼▲▼

March 24

In the past, most Ivorians who came to the market place were afraid to touch the masks. They thought that they would die if they came into contact with them. To those people the masks were fetishes. For those of us who sell masks, however, we can touch them all we want. We don't give a damn. Even if they tell me there's a certain kind of mask that prevents you from sleeping at night, I could take it home with me and use it as a pillow. Because I don't believe in these things. You have to believe in something in order for it to be effective. If you don't believe in it, then nothing will ever happen to you.

Abdurrahman Madu, African art merchant, 1991.
From Christopher B. Steiner's *African Art in Transit,* 1994

▼▲▼▲▼▲▼▲▼▲▼▲▼

March 25

Hasty marriages bring hasty divorces.

Oromo of Ethiopia and Kenya proverb

Cross of Lalibela, Ethiopia

▼▲▼▲▼▲▼▲▼▲▼▲▼

March 26

While the Westerner asserts that character formation is the chief thing, he forgets that character is formed primarily through relations with other people, and that there is really no other way in which it can grow. Europeans assume that, given the right knowledge and ideas, personal relations can be left largely to take care of themselves, and this is perhaps the most fundamental difference in outlook between Africans and Europeans.

Jomo Kenyatta, first president of Kenya. From *Facing Mount Kenya*, 1938

▼▲▼▲▼▲▼▲▼▲▼▲▼

March 27

You can borrow a basket and a sieve; you cannot borrow a face.

Ovimbundu of Angola proverb on the irreplaceability of individuals

Victory Day, Angola

Ivory mortar for snuff tobacco of the Chôkwe of Angola, Zaire and Zambia

▼▲▼▲▼▲▼▲▼▲▼▲▼

March 28

●

Man is still backward because he is unable to speak one common language. Until he attains this human aspiration, which seems impossible, the expression of joy and sorrow, what is good and bad, beauty and ugliness, comfort and misery, mortality and eternity, love and hatred, the description of colors, sentiments, tastes, and moods—all will be according to the language each people speaks.

Colonel Moammar Gadhafi, *The Green Book*, 1975–1981

Evacuation Day (commemorates the withdrawal of British troops from Libya at the end of World War II, which ended allied occupation of the country), Libya

Safari Rally (motor car race held from Good Friday to Easter Monday each year), Kenya

▼▲▼▲▼▲▼▲▼▲▼▲▼

March 29

Justice is like fire, even if you cover it with a veil, it still burns.

proverb from Madagascar

Memorial Day (commemorates the 1947 rebellion), Madagascar
Boganda Day (anniversary of the death of the first president), Central African Republic

▼▲▼▲▼▲▼▲▼▲▼▲▼

March 30

Ukimcheka mtoto mchanga akijamba, basi utajamba mwenyewe ya watu utatahayari sana.

If you laugh at a baby breaking wind you will accidentally do so yourself in the presence of people whom you respect.

Swahili of East Africa superstition

▼▲▼▲▼▲▼▲▼▲▼▲▼

March 31

Sit down when thou art taken by the hand and when thou receivest presents; and not when they lay hold of thy leg and drag thee away.

Egyptian proverb advising one to visit only when welcomed

Family Day, South Africa

April 1

The Oba of Benin

He who knows not the Oba
*   let me show him.*
He has mounted the throne,
*   he has piled a throne upon a throne.*
Plentiful as grains of sand on the earth
*   are those in front of him.*
There are two thousand people
*   to fan him.*
He who owns you
*   is among you here.*
He who owns you
*   has piled a throne upon a throne.*
He has lived to do it this year;
*   even so he will live to do it again.*

Traditional Bini of Nigeria poem

▼▲▼▲▼▲▼▲▼▲▼▲▼

April 2

Maasai of East Africa riddle:
    Who has more courage than a Maasai warrior?

Answer: Two Maasai warriors.

41

▼▲▼▲▼▲▼▲▼▲▼▲▼

April 3

Work is good, provided you do not forget to live.

African proverb

Brazzaville to Pointe-Noire Car Rally, Central Africa, held in early April (dates vary)
Human Rights Day, Guinea

▼▲▼▲▼▲▼▲▼▲▼▲▼

April 4

The civilization of the twentieth century cannot be universal except by being a dynamic synthesis of all the cultural values of all civilizations. It will be monstrous unless it is seasoned with the salt of negritude. For it will be the saviour of humanity.

Léopold Sédar Senghor, first president of Senegal. From an address to the Ghanaian Parliament, February 1961

National Day, Senegal

▼▲▼▲▼▲▼▲▼▲▼▲▼

April 5

Nothing could have been deader than Jesus on the cross that first Good Friday. And the hopes of his disciples had appeared to die with his crucifixion. Nothing could have been deeper than the despair of his followers when they saw their Master hanging on the Cross like a common criminal. The darkness that covered the earth for three hours during that Friday symbolized the blackness of their despair.

And then Easter happened. Jesus rose from the dead. The incredible, the unexpected happened. Life triumphed over death, light over darkness, love over hatred, good over evil. That is what Easter means—hope prevails over despair. Jesus reigns as Lord of Lords and King of Kings. Oppression and injustice and suffering can't be the end of the human story. Freedom and justice, peace and reconciliation, are his will for all of us, black and white, in this land and throughout the world. Easter says to us that despite everything to the contrary, his will for us will prevail, love will prevail over hate, justice over injustice and oppression, peace over exploitation and bitterness.

> Archbishop Desmond Tutu of South Africa, "An Easter Message"

▼▲▼▲▼▲▼▲▼▲▼▲▼

April 6

South Africa's oldest city, Cape Town, has long been known as the "tavern of the oceans." And indeed the country's position midway between the Orient and the Occident made it an ideal meeting-place for people and ideas from both hemispheres.

Modern-day South Africa has often been called the laboratory of mankind...a place where all races on earth are represented and live cheek by jowl.

> Piet Müller, South African journalist. From *Insight Guides South Africa*, 1992

Founders' Day (founding of Cape Town), South Africa
Patriots' Victory Day (celebrates end of Italian occupation in 1941), Ethiopia
Uprising Day (anniversary of the 1985 coup), Sudan

▼▲▼▲▼▲▼▲▼▲▼▲▼

April 7

Song of the Mozambican Women

Lifting her eyes to the certainty of victory,
Knowing that victory was built through sacrifice—
Who is it?
She who lifts high the beacon of freedom,
Who cries to the whole world
That our struggle is the same—
It's the emancipated Mozambican woman
Who brings her courage to the People.

Day of the Mozambican Woman, Mozambique

▼▲▼▲▼▲▼▲▼▲▼▲▼

April 8

In a few years there will be only five kings in the world—the King
of England and the four kings in a pack of cards.

King Farouk I of Egypt, *Life*, April 10, 1950

Mask of the Makonde of Mozambique

▼▲▼▲▼▲▼▲▼▲▼▲▼

April 9

Like pouring salt on a slug.

> Tunisian expression for a bad situation that is being made
> worse

Martyrs' Day, Tunisia

▼▲▼▲▼▲▼▲▼▲▼▲▼

April 10

To whom does God belong? Who has not the right to love Him or to scoff at Him? Think it over. . . . the freedom to love God or hate Him is God's ultimate gift, which no one takes from man.

> Cheikh Hamidou Kane, Senegalese writer. From *Ambiguous
> Adventure*, 1962

▼▲▼▲▼▲▼▲▼▲▼▲▼

April 11

THE TIDE AND THE MINNOW
A Vai of Liberia Folktale

One day, the Tide approached a minnow and asked, "What time does the moon change?" The Minnow said, "I haven't time to talk to you. I'm thirsty and need to get a drink of water." The Tide persisted, "Minnow, why are you behaving foolishly? You talk about being thirsty while you live in the water." The Minnow replied, "That is true, but you asked me when the moon changes. You are up when the moon is up; you are directly related to the moon. So now who behaves foolishly?"

Fast and Prayer Day, Liberia

▼▲▼▲▼▲▼▲▼▲▼▲▼

April 12

The frog says, "I have nothing, but I have my hop."

Vai of Liberia proverb describing those who are poor but proud
of what they have

National Redemption Day (anniversary of the 1980 coup), Liberia

▼▲▼▲▼▲▼▲▼▲▼▲▼

April 13

On the heels of the rainbow the people in the west know the rain is
too late and too brief to be of any real significance; it is too late.
They run in delirious circles nevertheless, to collect what they can
in buckets, in old milk tins, anything that will hold water. The
wells will run again, they will survive this year. They say a prayer
perhaps for those who did not last long enough to be able to say
this.

In the South the fields of war are silenced by rain. The drops
clatter down like the rattle of bones in a grey mist of moving
ghosts, like the echo of laughter, like the shadow of weeping.

In the offices of the government the clerks and the *murrasalas* are
thankful because once more the hand of God has intervened and
saved them the trouble of doing anything. They sit down and order
more tea.

Jamal Mahjoub, Sudanese writer. From *Navigation of a
Rainmaker*, 1989

▼▲▼▲▼▲▼▲▼▲▼▲▼

April 14

The mist of the coast is the rain upland.

Ovimbundu of Angola proverb equivalent to "One man's meat
is another man's poison"

▼▲▼▲▼▲▼▲▼▲▼▲▼

April 15

Profit is profit, even in Mecca.

Hausa of West Africa proverb

Anniversary of the 1974 Coup, Niger

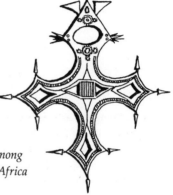

Cross design popular among
Hausa women of West Africa

▼▲▼▲▼▲▼▲▼▲▼▲▼

April 16

We ignore man's basic nature if we say...that because a man...had risen overnight from poverty and insignificance to his present opulence he could be persuaded without much trouble to give it up again and return to his original state.

A man who has just come in from the rain and dried his body and put on dry clothes is more reluctant to go out again than another who has been indoors all the time. The trouble with our new nation...was that none of us had been indoors long enough....We had all been in the rain together until yesterday. Then a handful of us—the smart and the lucky and hardly ever the best—had scrambled for the one shelter our former rulers left, and had taken it over and barricaded themselves in. And from within

they sought to persuade the rest through numerous loudspeakers
...that all argument should cease and the whole people speak
with one voice and that any more dissent and argument outside
the door of the shelter would subvert and bring down the whole
house.

> Chinua Achebe, Nigerian writer. From *A Man of the People*,
> 1966, Achebe's classic novel about a newly independent African
> nation

▼▲▼▲▼▲▼▲▼▲▼▲▼

April 17

A rose fell to the lot of the monkey.

> Egyptian expression for those who are believed to be
> undeserving of their good luck

Sham an-Nessim (Coptic Easter Monday), Egypt, Sudan (date varies)

▼▲▼▲▼▲▼▲▼▲▼▲▼

April 18

*Your Majesty, what I want to know from you is if people can be bought
at any price....*
*Your Majesty, what I want to know from you is: Why do your people
kill me?*
*Do you kill me for following my stolen cattle which are seen in the
possession of the Mashonas....*
*I have called all white men living at or near Bulawayo to hear my
words, showing clearly that I am not hiding anything from them
when writing to Your Majesty.*

> Chief Lobengula, last Matabele king. From a letter to Queen
> Victoria

Independence Day, Zimbabwe

▼▲▼▲▼▲▼▲▼▲▼▲▼

April 19

There was no sky as totally black as an African sky, where the stars hung so low that one could almost reach out to pluck them from the heavens.

> Farida Karodia, South African writer. From *A Shattering of Silence*, 1993

King's Birthday (Mswati III), Swaziland

▼▲▼▲▼▲▼▲▼▲▼▲▼

April 20

It was a small dog, a Japanese breed....During various ceremonies, he would run away from the Emperor's lap and pee on dignitaries' shoes. The august gentlemen were not allowed to flinch or make the slightest gesture when they felt their feet getting wet. I had to walk among the dignitaries and wipe urine from their shoes with a satin cloth. This was my job for ten years.

> One of the many minor officials in the court of Haile Selassie, emperor of Ethiopia, explains his job to Polish journalist Ryszard Kapuscinski in his book *The Emperor: Downfall Of an Autocrat*, 1983

▼▲▼▲▼▲▼▲▼▲▼▲▼

April 21

Do not boast of your knowledge,
but seek the advice of the untutored
as much as the well educated.

> Advice from "Instructions of Ptahhotep," an ancient Egyptian text written during the Fifth Dynasty (2565–2420 B.C.)

▼▲▼▲▼▲▼▲▼▲▼▲▼

April 22

THE BLIND MAN AND THE LAMP
A Hausa of West Africa Folktale

A boy was out walking at night when he rounded a corner and
nearly bumped into a man who was carrying a lamp. The boy saw
it was a blind man. "Blind man," said the boy, "how bothersome
you are! What has driven you to wander at night with a lamp? Day
and night make no difference to you." The blind man replied,
"That is true, they are the same to me. But in both I still have more
sense than you: I carry this lamp not for myself, but for fools like
you so you don't collide with me."

▼▲▼▲▼▲▼▲▼▲▼▲▼

April 23

The snake flees from the man; the man flees from the snake, and
the road remains empty. Thus does enmity waste opportunity.

Oromo of Ethiopia and Kenya proverb

*Small bronze mask representing the face of an enemy
killed in battle of the Baule of Côte d'Ivoire*

▼▲▼▲▼▲▼▲▼▲▼▲▼

April 24

I put a date in his mouth, and he puts a stick in my eye!

Tunisian expression for ingratitude

Victory Day, Togo

▼▲▼▲▼▲▼▲▼▲▼▲▼

April 25

Any life that is lost in war is a human life, be it that of an Arab or an Israeli. A wife who becomes a widow is a human being entitled to a happy family life, whether she be an Arab or an Israeli. Innocent children who are deprived of the care and compassion of their parents are ours. They are ours, be they living on Arab or Israeli land.

Anwar Sadat, third president of Egypt. From a speech delivered before the Israeli Knesset in 1977

Sinai Liberation Day, Egypt
National Flag Day, Swaziland

▼▲▼▲▼▲▼▲▼▲▼▲▼

April 26

The individual is part of the conscious human race or he is an animal grubbing for sustenance.

Julius K. Nyerere, first president of Tanzania

Union Day (National Day), Tanzania

▼▲▼▲▼▲▼▲▼▲▼▲▼

April 27

There is no easy walk to freedom anywhere and many of us will have to pass through the valley of the shadow of death and again before we reach the mountain tops of our desires.

Nelson Mandela, president of South Africa

To give up the task of reforming society is to give up one's responsibility as a free man.

Alan Paton, South African writer, 1967

Freedom Day, South Africa
Independence Day, Sierra Leone, Togo

▼▲▼▲▼▲▼▲▼▲▼▲▼

April 28

One falsehood spoils a thousand truths.

Ashanti of Ghana proverb

Fertility doll of the Ashanti of Ghana

▼▲▼▲▼▲▼▲▼▲▼▲▼

April 29

The twenty-ninth or thirtieth... all try to be the first to discover the new moon.... the new moon must be clearly seen before the fast can be said to be at an end....

Keen-eyed men are sent up to the roof of the fort (a remnant of the Portuguese dominion) and to the mastheads of our ships to signal the first approach of the silvery crook....

At last a crash shakes our building from roof to basement, and immediately on that follow cries of joy from every soul in the town, with the words "Id mbarak" (a happy feast to you).

The first gun is fired at six o'clock, to be followed by the firing of a succession of shots in honour of the Feast of the Faithful; if there are any foreign men-of-war in the port, they also fire a salute of twenty-one guns. Every Arab shows his joy on such a day by letting off as many fireworks as he can—a stranger might almost fancy himself in a bombarded city.

Emily Ruete, *Memoirs of an Arabian Princess from Zanzibar*, 1989.
Ruete describes the opening of the festival, which marks the
end of the holy month of Ramadan as it occurred on the island
of Zanzibar around the turn of the century.

▼▲▼▲▼▲▼▲▼▲▼▲▼

April 30

Mwenye kuzowea kula ndani ya chungu atapata mvua kubwa siku ya harusi yake.

One who eats straight from the cooking pot will have heavy rain on his wedding day.

Swahili of East Africa superstition

▼▲▼▲▼▲▼▲▼▲▼▲▼

May 1

One may work from necessity, for the cessation of the great pain of need which wells up from the body and from the earth—to impose silence on all those voices which harass us with their demands. Then, too, one works to maintain oneself, to preserve the species. But one can also work from greed. In this case, one is not trying to block off the pit of need; that has been wholly filled already. One is not even seeking to defer the next date when that need's claim will come due. One accumulates frantically, believing that in multiplying riches one multiplies life. Finally, one can work from a mania for working—I do not say to distract oneself, it is more frenzied than that; one works like a stereotype. It is with work as with the sexual act: both are aimed at the perpetuation of the species; but both may have their perversion when they do not justify themselves to this aim.

Chiekh Hamidou Kane, Senegalese writer. From *Ambiguous
Adventure*, 1962

Labor Day, observed throughout Africa
Id al-Adha, Muslim holiday (date varies)

▼▲▼▲▼▲▼▲▼▲▼▲▼

May 2

I'm working in hunger,
The owners are full:
It's a bad sign,
It's a bad sign.

Mozambican work song

King's Birthday, Lesotho

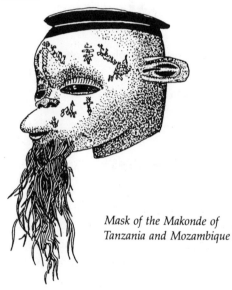

Mask of the Makonde of
Tanzania and Mozambique

▼▲▼▲▼▲▼▲▼▲▼▲▼

May 3

When he woke up the sun was already three hours old, blazing on
the township scene. He whipped open the thin curtains and
looked outside. A group of young boys were playing football in the
street. An ice-cream man and a firewood vendor were jangling

their bells from the opposite ends of the road. Young girls sauntered from the grocer's with loaves of bread or packets of milk, neat little green packages of meat and bottles of paraffin, frugal tots of cooking oil and bunches of chaoumoellier. A mother with a blanket round her waist was slapping a naked child playing with a garden tap. The child was screaming wildly and stamping her feet.

Shimmer Chinodya, Zimbabwean writer. From Harvest of
Thorns, 1989

▼▲▼▲▼▲▼▲▼▲▼▲▼

May 4

Good is when I steal other people's wives and cattle; bad is when they steal mine.

Hottentot of southern Africa proverb

Cassinga Day (commemorates the struggle against South African rule), Namibia

▼▲▼▲▼▲▼▲▼▲▼▲▼

May 5

Most people seek after what they do not possess and are thus enslaved by the very things they want to acquire.

Only when he has ceased to need things can a man truly be his own master and so really exist.

Anwar Sadat, third president of Egypt. From In Search of
Identity, 1978

▼▲▼▲▼▲▼▲▼▲▼▲▼

May 6

Musakangaze kumeza pamene kutafuna kuli kokoma.

Don't be in a hurry to swallow when chewing is pleasant.

Nyanja of Malawi proverb

▼▲▼▲▼▲▼▲▼▲▼▲▼

May 7

THE MAKING OF THE RACES
An Ethiopian Folktale

When God was creating the heavens and the earth he decided to make people out of dough. He put the human cutouts in the oven to bake. The first batch, he didn't cook long enough. They came out pasty and white, so he threw them to the north of the world where they became the people of Europe. With the second batch, he overcompensated and left them in the oven too long. This batch became quite black and burnt, so he threw them southward where they became the Bantu people of Africa. By the third batch he had everything just right. The people came out a luscious golden brown. God took these people in the palm of his hand and gently set them down at the top of the world—in Ethiopia.

Fasika (Easter Sunday), Ethiopia, Eritrea (date varies)

▼▲▼▲▼▲▼▲▼▲▼▲▼

May 8

If I should find my friend in the wrong, I reproach him secretly; but in the presence of company, I praise him.... Advice given in the midst of a crowd is loathsome.

Egyptian maxim

▼▲▼▲▼▲▼▲▼▲▼▲▼▲▼

May 9

Reconciliation is no easy option, nor does it rule out confrontation. After all, it did cost God the death of His Son to effect reconciliation; the cross of Jesus was to expose the sinfulness of sin when He took on the powers of evil and routed them comprehensively. No, just as there can be no cheap grace so there can be no cheap reconciliation, because we cannot cry "peace, peace" where there is no peace.

> Archbishop Desmond Tutu of South Africa, "Politics and
> Religion—The Seamless Garment" from *Hope and Suffering*,
> 1994

▼▲▼▲▼▲▼▲▼▲▼▲▼▲▼

May 10

Work on your reputation until it is established; when it is established it will work for you.

> Tunisian proverb

Id al-Adha (Feast of the Sacrifice), observed in Muslim countries and communities across Africa (date varies)

▼▲▼▲▼▲▼▲▼▲▼▲▼▲▼

May 11

He came through the idyllic gardens of the savannah and saw the pageant of the migratory birds going back to Europe with their impertinent looks and their fanciful plumages. Not having been in that part of the world for a while, he strayed into the sandy desolation of the desert, to see what changes the discovery of the compass had made since the days of the camel. His patience was rewarded: on the vast plateau in the awesome silence of the sand, Alusine Dunbar saw the majestic castles and caves of Tassili n'Ajir, the fantastic drawings of the nomadic painters; he rested on the stones in the rock garden of antiquity and read the epigram, "Gold is the king of jewels but do not love it more than the sands of the desert...."

Syl Cheney-Coker, Sierra Leonean writer. From *The Last Harmattan of Alusine Dunbar,* 1990

▼▲▼▲▼▲▼▲▼▲▼▲▼

May 12

The rain does not befriend anybody; it falls on anyone it meets outside.

Yoruba of Nigeria proverb on the leveling power of nature

Ibeji statuette of the Yoruba of nigeria

▼▲▼▲▼▲▼▲▼▲▼▲▼

May 13

"Young man," he said, "go after property. But never show God your nakedness, and never despise the people. The voice of the people is the voice of God."

Ngugi wa Thiong'o, Kenyan writer

▼▲▼▲▼▲▼▲▼▲▼▲▼

May 14

We were here when trouble came to our people;
For this reason Yancy came to our country—
He caught our husbands and our brothers,
Sail them to 'Nana Poo
And there they die!
And there they die!

Tell us
Yancy, why?
Yancy, why?
Wadebo women have no husbands,
Yancy, why?
Wadebo women have no brothers,
Yancy, why?
Mothers, fathers, sons have died,
Waiting for the return
Yancy, why?

Wadebo of Liberia song referring to boys being sent into forced labor on the island of Fernando Po in the early 1900s; Allen N. Yancy was the vice president of Liberia at the time

National Unification Day, Liberia

▼▲▼▲▼▲▼▲▼▲▼▲▼

May 15

A nation that refuses to keep its rendezvous with history, that does not believe to be the bearer of a unique message—that nation is finished, ready to be placed in a museum....Let the Negro African speak: above all, let him act. Let him bring like a leaven his message to the world in order to help build a universal civilization.

Léopold Sédar Senghor, first president of Senegal

▼▲▼▲▼▲▼▲▼▲▼▲▼

May 16

May the days kill me, that I perish!
May the years kill me, that I perish!
I call out "woe!"
I call the days!
Years—I do not believe that I shall live them.
Days—I do not believe that I shall live them.
Any measure of time—I do not believe that I shall live it.

Bergdama of Namibia chant

▼▲▼▲▼▲▼▲▼▲▼▲▼

May 17

There's one thing I'm sure of—hell or paradise, we'll never get out
of it.

Driss Chraibi, Moroccan writer. From *Heirs to the Past,* 1962

Mūt l-ard (first day of summer), Morocco

▼▲▼▲▼▲▼▲▼▲▼▲▼

May 18

We lived in freedom
Before man appeared:
Our world was undisturbed,
One day followed the other joyfully,
Dissent was never heard.
    Then man broke into our forest
    With cunning and belligerence,
    He pursued us
    With greed and envy:
Our freedom vanished.

"Song of the Turtle," traditional Ghanaian poem

▼▲▼▲▼▲▼▲▼▲▼▲▼

May 19

A thousand raps at the door, but no salute or invitation from within.

> Egyptian expression for when a person is unsuccessful at
> becoming intimate with another

▼▲▼▲▼▲▼▲▼▲▼▲▼

May 20

One of our people, one of our people, it's easy enough to say that. Human beings are not all the same. There are good men and there are crooks among our people, the same as everywhere else.

> Mongo Beti, Cameroonian writer. From *Perpetua and the Habit
> of Unhappiness*, 1974

National Day, Cameroon
MPR Day (anniversary of the Mouvement Populaire de la Révolution), Zaire

Big-cheeked mask from Cameroon

▼▲▼▲▼▲▼▲▼▲▼▲▼

May 21

Hausa of West Africa Riddle:
  Why is a man like pepper?

Answer: Until you have tested him, you can't tell how strong he is.

▼▲▼▲▼▲▼▲▼▲▼▲▼

May 22

When the missionaries came, we had the land and they had the Bible. They taught us to pray with our eyes closed. When we opened them, they had the land and we had the Bible.

  Jomo Kenyatta, first president of Kenya

▼▲▼▲▼▲▼▲▼▲▼▲▼

May 23

If you find them worshipping a donkey, bring him grass.

  Moroccan proverb advising one to respect other peoples' customs. Equivalent to our "When in Rome, do as the Romans do"

National Holiday, Morocco

▼▲▼▲▼▲▼▲▼▲▼▲▼

May 24

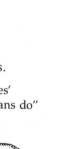

Do not hurry the night, the sun will always rise for its own sake.

  Eritrean expression

Independence Day, Eritrea

Coffee pot from Eritrea

▼▲▼▲▼▲▼▲▼▲▼▲▼

May 25

You are either alive and proud or you are dead, and when you are dead, you don't care anyway. And your method of death can itself be a politicizing thing. So you die in the riots. For a hell of a lot of them, in fact, there's really nothing to lose—almost literally, given the kind of situations they come from. So if you can overcome the personal fear of death, which is a highly irrational thing, you know, then you're on the way.

Steve Biko, South African political activist. From *I Write What I Like*, 1978

Africa Freedom Day (anniversary of the founding of the Organization of African Unity), observed in many countries

▼▲▼▲▼▲▼▲▼▲▼▲▼

May 26

What the family talks about in the evening, the child will talk about in the morning.

Oromo of Ethiopia and Kenya proverb

Mother's Day, Gabon (last Sunday in May)

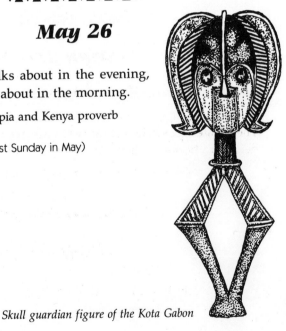

Skull guardian figure of the Kota Gabon

▼▲▼▲▼▲▼▲▼▲▼▲▼

May 27

Ukiona mwasho juu ya kiganja cha mkono wa kulia utapokea fedha. Kiganja cha mkono wa kushoto kikikuwasha ni alama ya kutumia fedha.

If you feel an itching on your right palm it means that you will receive money. If you feel an itching on your left palm it means you will spend money.

Swahili of East Africa superstition

▼▲▼▲▼▲▼▲▼▲▼▲▼

May 28

If you want sex while traveling, travel with your wife.

Minyanka of Mali proverb

▼▲▼▲▼▲▼▲▼▲▼▲▼

May 29

The greatest obstacle to love is fear. It has been the source of all defects in human behaviour throughout the ages.

Mahmoud Mohammed Taha, Sudanese reformer

▼▲▼▲▼▲▼▲▼▲▼▲▼

May 30

Peace is costly, but it is worth the expense.

Kikuyu of Kenya proverb

▼▲▼▲▼▲▼▲▼▲▼▲▼

May 31

History, like beauty, depends largely on the beholder, so when you read that, for example, David Livingstone discovered the Victoria Falls, you might be forgiven for thinking that there was nobody around the Falls until Livingstone arrived on the scene.

Archbishop Desmond Tutu, on the twentieth anniversary of
the Republic of South Africa, 1981

Islamic New Year, observed in Muslim countries and communities across Africa (date varies)

Helmet mask from western Sudan

▼▲▼▲▼▲▼▲▼▲▼▲▼

June 1

Civilised or not civilised, ignorant or illiterate, rich or poor, we, the African States, deserve a government of our own choice. Let us make our own mistakes, but let us at least take comfort in the knowledge that they are our own mistakes.

Tom Mboya, Kenyan nationalist leader

Madaraka Day (anniversary of self-government), Kenya

▼▲▼▲▼▲▼▲▼▲▼▲▼

June 2

Likawomba wotha. (Mawa kuli mitambo.)

While it shines, bask! (Tomorrow there may be clouds.)

Nyanja of Malawi proverb

▼▲▼▲▼▲▼▲▼▲▼▲▼

June 3

Another path, which conveniently twists as if in conformity with the often unsteady feet that stumble along it, brings you to the Happy Bar, the tin-roofed dwelling where Maria Ssentamu's sumptuous curves shake in perpetual merriment as she serves warm beer in thick, greasy glasses to the thirsty locals. Maria must

67

surely weigh over fourteen stones. Nevertheless, she is by far the most seductive woman in the village, and she has a number of children to prove it. It seems that a simple shake of her magnificent hips is enough to bowl a man over. Few can withstand the onslaught. Members of the Mothers Union spitefully whisper that this unfailing charm is all something to do with what Maria puts in the drinks.

Barbara Kimenye, Ugandan writer. From *The Village*, 1965

Martyrs' Day, Uganda

▼▲▼▲▼▲▼▲▼▲▼▲▼

June 4

If you see someone riding a log, tell him what a beautiful horse.

Tunisian expression advising to let others enjoy their own fantasies

▼▲▼▲▼▲▼▲▼▲▼▲▼

June 5

Haraka, haraka, haina baraka.

Haste, haste, doesn't bring blessings.

Swahili of East Africa proverb

Liberation Day (anniversary of the 1977 coup), Seychelles

▼▲▼▲▼▲▼▲▼▲▼▲▼

June 6

Jicho Na Moyo

Jicho ndilo la awali
mashaka kukuletea
moyo ukawa wa pili
matatani kukutia
adui hawa wawili
walaumu wote pia.

Macho hufuata dili
wazuri kuwavumbua
na moyo bila suali

hupenda na kuchukua
nawe hufunui kweli

mapenzi kuyachagua.

Jicho halitakubali
mzuri kutovumbua

moyo kwake ni thakili
mapenzi kuyaachia.
Moyo hauna akili
jicho halina pazia.

Mkarara

Laumu vyote viwili
usilaumu kimoja.

The Eye and the Heart

The eye was the first
to give you trouble,
and the heart was the second
to entangle you.
These two are the enemy,
blame them both.

The eyes follow the heart
to discover the beautiful ones,
and the heart, without further
question,
loves and takes;
and you do not really
consciously
choose your love.

The eye will not agree
not to discover a beautiful
one;
it is hard for the heart
to relinquish love.
The heart has no brain,
the eye has no curtain.

Refrain

Blame both of them,
do not blame just one.

Swahili love poem

▼▲▼▲▼▲▼▲▼▲▼▲▼▲▼

June 7

If God dishes your rice in a basket you should not wish to eat soup.

Mende of Sierra Leone proverb advising to be content with
one's lot in life

▼▲▼▲▼▲▼▲▼▲▼▲▼▲▼

June 8

THE MAN WHO NEVER ATTENDED PUBLIC GATHERINGS
A Kalenjin of Kenya Folktale

Long ago, men used to raid neighboring tribes to steal cattle. The
elders would gather the warriors together before each raid to
discuss plans and strategies. One particularly strong warrior never
bothered to attend these gatherings because he thought there was
nothing new he needed to learn.

One day, the elders summoned the warriors to discuss an
upcoming raid that required crossing the land of ruthless monster.
They planned to outwit the monster by having each warrior tell
the monster to wait for the person coming behind because that
warrior was much stronger.

On the day the warriors entered the monster's territory, the
warrior who never attended public gatherings was bringing up the
rear. The men in front passed by the monster easily, so the warrior
in the rear assumed he also would pass without being harmed. As
he approached the monster, the creature ordered the warrior to
carry him across the path. The man who never attended public
gatherings said: "All those strong warriors have gone by and you
didn't ask them to carry you across." The monster replied: "That's
because they told me the strongest one was coming behind." "That
is true," conceded the warrior. "Climb on." The monster jumped
on top of the man who never attended public gatherings and ate
him bones and all. From that day forward no one missed any
public gatherings.

▼▲▼▲▼▲▼▲▼▲▼▲▼

June 9

Really to most Ugandans the coup was a relief. As you know, in African States there will never be a perfect government. Always we hope that the coming government will be better than the previous one.

Ugandan child's comments on the coup of July 1985

National Heroes' Day, Uganda

▼▲▼▲▼▲▼▲▼▲▼▲▼

June 10

When the cock crows,
The lazy man smacks his lips, and says:
So it is daylight again is it?
before he turns over heavily.

Yoruba of Nigeria poem

▼▲▼▲▼▲▼▲▼▲▼▲▼

June 11

The eye crosses the river before the body.

Ndebele of Zimbabwe proverb equivalent to our "Don't count your chickens before they hatch"

Evacuation Day, Libya

▼▲▼▲▼▲▼▲▼▲▼▲▼

June 12

Do not set pen on papyrus to cheat a man,
For it is hateful to God.

Do not bear false witness with lying words,
Nor lend your tongue to support the perjury of another.

Make no accounting against one who has nothing,
For it falsifies a man's pen.

Advice from the "Teaching of Amen-em-opet," an ancient
Egyptian text believed to have been written during the
Nineteenth Dynasty, c. 1200 B.C.

▼▲▼▲▼▲▼▲▼▲▼▲▼

June 13

Aan wada hadalno waa aan heshiino.

Where there is negotiation, there is hope for agreement.

Somali proverb

Independence Day, Djibouti

▼▲▼▲▼▲▼▲▼▲▼▲▼

June 14

Ukalemera vinila m'nyumba.

If you should become rich, dance in the house.

> Nyanja of Malawi proverb discouraging boastful behavior

Freedom Day, Malawi

▼▲▼▲▼▲▼▲▼▲▼▲▼

June 15

If an onion causes his loud rejoices, what then shall we say to sugar?

> Egyptian expression for those who gush with admiration over trivial things

▼▲▼▲▼▲▼▲▼▲▼▲▼

June 16

"Age ain't nothin' but a number." But age is other things, too. It is wisdom, if one has lived one's life properly. It is experience and knowledge. And it is getting to know all the ways the world turns, so that if you cannot turn the world the way you want, you can at least get out of the way so you won't get run over.

> Miriam Makeba, South African singer and political activist.
> From *Makeba, My Story*, 1987

Youth Day, South Africa
Father's Day, Gabon (second Sunday in June)

▼▲▼▲▼▲▼▲▼▲▼▲▼

June 17

To look at green adorns the heart and the eye.

Moroccan proverb acknowledging the importance of natural
surroundings

▼▲▼▲▼▲▼▲▼▲▼▲▼

June 18

In every facet of our lives—in politics, in commerce and in the
professions—robbery is the base line. And it's been so from time.
In the early days, our forebears sold their kinsmen into slavery for
minor items such as beads, mirrors, alcohol and tobacco. These
days, the tune is the same, only the articles have changed into
cars, transistor radios and bank accounts. Nothing else has
changed, and nothing will change in the foreseeable future. But
that's the problem of those of you who will live beyond tomorrow.

Ken Saro-Wiwa, Nigerian writer. From "Africa Kills Her Sun"

▼▲▼▲▼▲▼▲▼▲▼▲▼

June 19

Although it is hard work it is also inspiring, and there is beauty in
the idea of transforming even a minute portion of the earth's
surface into fertile, productive soil.

Ahmed Ben Bella, first president of Algeria, 1965

This wonderful country had been at war for seven years and had
lost a million dead; it was still scarred and bleeding, and its people
were poverty-stricken. It had got to be rebuilt, on new founda-

tions, from top to bottom. Would fate allow me the time in which to do it?

Ben Bella, in an interview not long before being deposed in a coup on June 19, 1965

Anniversary of the Overthrow of Ben Bella, Algeria

▼▲▼▲▼▲▼▲▼▲▼▲▼▲▼

June 20

The old woman has a reason for running in the rice field.

Baule of Côte d'Ivoire expression about the wisdom of age

Martyrs' Day, Eritrea

Small bronze mask representing the face of an enemy killed in battle of the Baule of Côte d'Ivoire

▼▲▼▲▼▲▼▲▼▲▼▲▼▲▼

June 21

Dawn breaks when you come up over the horizon, for by day you are the Sun and dispel the darkness. You cast your rays and the Two Kingdoms bask in festive brilliance. People wake up and start to their feet; it is you who roused them. They wash themselves, pick up their clothes and raise their arms in praise of your appearance.

Eulogy to the Sun by Akhenaten, ancient Egyptian king

June 22

Umleavyo mtoto, ndivyo akuavyo.

The way you bring up a child is the way it grows up.

Swahili proverb

June 23

THE JACKAL AND THE HERON
A Hausa of West Africa Fable

One day a jackal was eating a chicken when a bone got caught in his throat. The jackal cried out for someone to help dislodge the bone, and offered his rescuer a big reward. The grey heron came forward, stuck its head in the jackal's mouth, and with its long bill extracted the bone. The jackal turned to go on its way. The heron said, "Wait a minute. Where's my reward?" The jackal replied, "Your reward is this: you put your head in my mouth and got away safely."

June 24

Great events may stem from words of no importance.

You do not teach the paths of the forest to an old gorilla.

Zairean proverbs

Zaire Day (anniversary of Zaire currency and promulgation of the 1967
constitution, and day of the fishermen), Zaire

Bowl of the Luba of Zaire

▼▲▼▲▼▲▼▲▼▲▼▲▼

June 25

A State of rich and powerful men in which a minority decides and
imposes its will, whether we agree or not, and whether we
understand or not, would be the continuation in a new form of the
situation against which we are struggling. The question of people's power is the essential question of our revolution.

Samora Moises Machel, first president of Mozambique

Independence Day, Mozambique

▼▲▼▲▼▲▼▲▼▲▼▲▼

June 26

Watching Europe burn with its
civilization of fire,
Watching America disintegrate
with its gods of steel,
Watching the persecutors of
mankind turn into dust,
Was I wrong? Was I wrong?

Mazisi Kunene, South African poet, excerpt from "Thought on
June 26," *Zulu Poems,* 1970.

▼▲▼▲▼▲▼▲▼▲▼▲▼

June 27

The British, the Ethiopians and the Italians
are squabbling,
The country is snatched and divided by
whoever is stronger,
The country is sold piece by piece
without our knowledge,
And for me, all this is the teeth of
the last days of the world.

Faarah Nuur, Somali poet and clan leader

Independence Day, Somalia
Independence Day, Madagascar

▼▲▼▲▼▲▼▲▼▲▼▲▼

June 28

Mtu akijiuma anapokuwa anakula ni alama kuwa anatajwa.

If a person bites himself while eating it is a sign that someone is talking about him.

Swahili of East Africa superstition

▼▲▼▲▼▲▼▲▼▲▼▲▼

June 29

Everything bears both death and life. Rain brings down lightning and life-giving water, earth brings forth harvest and entombs the dead, the sun spreads light and drought; the years bring on old age and famine, children and Independence.

Ahmadou Kourouma, Ivorian writer. From The Suns of Independence, 1968

Independence Day, Seychelles

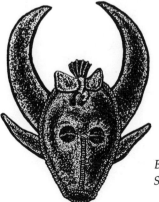

Bronze Bush cow ring of the Senufo of Côte d'Ivoire

▼▲▼▲▼▲▼▲▼▲▼▲▼

June 30

The shores of the great river, full of promises,
Henceforth belong to you.
This earth and all its riches
Henceforth belong to you.
And the fiery sun, high in the colorless sky,
Will burn away your pain
Its searing rays will forever dry
The tears your forefathers shed
Tormented by their tyrannical masters
On this soil that you still cherish.
And you will make the Congo a free and happy nation,
In the heart of this giant Black Africa.

Patrice Lumumba, nationalist leader of the Belgian Congo
(now Zaire). From *Weep, O Beloved Black Brother,* 1959

Independence Day, Zaire
National Day of Prayer, Central African Republic
Revolution Day, Sudan

July 1

If the palm of your hand itches, it signifies that great luck is coming your way.

Lesotho superstition

Family Day, Lesotho
Independence Day, Rwanda
Independence Day, Burundi
Republic Day (anniversary of self-government), Ghana
Decentralization Day, Sudan
Foundation of the Republic Day, Somalia

▼▲▼▲▼▲▼▲▼▲▼▲▼

July 2

My brother is there
I can hear the bells of his camels
When they graze down in the valley,
And the leaves of the bushes they browse at
Have the same sweetness as the bushes near my place
Because the rain which
Makes them grow comes from the same sky.
When I pray, he prays,
And my Allah is his Allah.
My brother is there
And he cannot come to me.

Anonymous Somali poem. The poet regrets being unable to cross the border after Somalia loses a war with neighboring Ethiopia

▼▲▼▲▼▲▼▲▼▲▼▲▼

July 3

You know that if everyone in the world were equally sophisticated, the world would chew itself up. We can't all have the same amount of intelligence.... There will always be a certain number of ignorant people. There are those with their eyes open and those with their eyes closed. If we all had our eyes open—if you knew everything that I knew—things just wouldn't work. It's like a scale; as one end goes up, the other end necessarily must go back down.... If everyone knew the same thing, then there would be no market.

> Abdurraham Madu, African art merchant, 1991. From
> Christopher B. Steiner's *African Art in Transit*, 1994

▼▲▼▲▼▲▼▲▼▲▼▲▼

July 4

The smile of a dog and the deeds of God, one does not understand.

Oromo of Ethiopia and Kenya proverb

*Hand weapon (variant of the "toucan beak" design)
of the Mbede of Gabon*

▼▲▼▲▼▲▼▲▼▲▼▲▼

July 5

War is just like bush-clearing—the moment you stop, the jungle comes back even thicker, but for a little while you can plant and grow a crop in the ground you have won at such a terrible cost.

Kenneth Kaunda, first president of Zambia. From *Kaunda on Violence*, 1980

Heroes' Day, Zambia
Independence Day, Algeria
Independence Day, Cape Verde

▼▲▼▲▼▲▼▲▼▲▼▲▼

July 6

I wish that I could bring Stonehenge to Nyasaland, to show that there was a time when Britain had a savage culture.

Hastings Banda, first president of Malawi (formerly Nyasaland), *The Observer*, March 10, 1963

Republic Day, Malawi
Independence Day, Comoros

▼▲▼▲▼▲▼▲▼▲▼▲▼

July 7

Whoever imposes oppression, however large or small the number of victims, and however understandable the feelings of fear or revenge which promote it, racial discrimination is the mother of war, and suffering, and loss of freedom for everyone. For if men cannot live as men they will at least die as men.

Julius K. Nyerere, first president of Tanzania

Saba Saba (International Trade Fair Day), Tanzania

▼▲▼▲▼▲▼▲▼▲▼▲▼

July 8

Machozi Ya Huba

Tears of Love

Machozi ya huba
yamenidondoka
sili nikashiba
nikafurahika
wangu mahububu
ameshanitoka.

Tears of love
trickle down my face,
I do not eat enough
and it pleases me not.
My beloved
has deserted me.

Ameshanitoka
mpenzi jamini
msitu na nyika
chozi kifuani
ninahangaika
wala simuoni

She has deserted me,
my darling, comrades!
The forest and the savannah,
a sob in my throat.
I am distraught
for I do not see her.

Wala simuoni
sijui aliko
anipa mashaka
na masikitiko.
Sauti naghani
ajue niliko.

I do not see her,
I do not know where she is,
she gives me sorrow,
and regret.
I sing with all my voice
so that she may know where I am.

Old Swahili love song

Unity Day, Zambia

▼▲▼▲▼▲▼▲▼▲▼▲▼

July 9

The speech of a man which is beautiful and understood is better than the speech of a thousand mouths that is not.

Moroccan proverb

Youth Day, Morocco

▼▲▼▲▼▲▼▲▼▲▼▲▼

July 10

THE IRON MAN
A Ugandan Folktale

There once was a Ugandan king who loved to own new and unusual things. One day this king summoned Walukaga, the kingdom's best blacksmith, and said, "I will supply all the materials you need, and you will create a breathing, walking, talking man—out of iron." The king's men then deposited a pile of iron bars at the blacksmith's feet. When Walukaga told his friends about the king's demand, they all responded the same way: "It is not possible. You must tell the king it can't be done." "No," said Walukaga, "if I refuse I will certainly lose my life."

Walukaga spent many days contemplating his dilemma. He discussed it with the elders, he consulted wise men, but none could help him. In despair, Walukaga set off towards the palace to inform the king of his failure. Along the road Walukaga was approached by a crazy man, who asked what was troubling him. The blacksmith confided the king's impossible request. "Has the king supplied you with charcoal and water for this man of iron?" asked the madman. "No, but he agreed to provide all necessary supplies." "This is no ordinary ironwork," said the madman. "You'll need special charcoal and water to produce a man. Ask the king for one hundred baskets of charcoal made from burned human hair and ten gourds filled with human tears to water the charcoal."

Walukaga presented himself to the king and said, "Great king, I praise you. I am ready to begin my task, but I will need some more supplies. I need one hundred baskets of charcoal made from human hair and ten gourds filled with human tears." Thus, the king decreed that everyone should shave the hair off their bodies and shed tears into containers. Throughout the kingdom, every man, woman, and child shaved and wept to fill their quota. The hair was gathered and burned to make charcoal, but it filled only one basket. All the people's tears could barely fill a gourd.

Disappointed, the king summoned Walukaga and said, "I am not able to provide the special charcoal and water you need, therefore you can cease trying to make a man of iron." After leaving the palace, Walukaga advised his friends: "Listen to everyone, not only the educated; even a crazy man sometimes says wise things."

▼▲▼▲▼▲▼▲▼▲▼▲▼

July 11

The truth must be told, however harsh it may be; it may redden your eyes, but it won't blind you.

Ahmadou Kourouma, Ivorian writer. From *The Suns of Independence*, 1968

Bronze weight of the Bamun of Côte

▼▲▼▲▼▲▼▲▼▲▼▲▼

July 12

Ii gwe Uthaaraga;	Oh, you who lights;
Njuu unthaarire;	Come and light for me;
Na uthaarire antu bakwa;	And light for my people;
Na into biakwa'	And for my property;
Na uthaarire antu bangi;	And light for other people;
Baria ukenda.	Those you may like.

Traditional Meru of Kenya poem in praise of the rising sun

Independence Day, São Tomé and Príncipe

▼▲▼▲▼▲▼▲▼▲▼▲▼

July 13

What is sensible today may be madness another time.

Yoruba of Nigeria proverb

Maiden spirit mask from Nigeria

▼▲▼▲▼▲▼▲▼▲▼▲▼

July 14

All day long along the long straight rails
(Unbending will on the listless sands)
Across the dryness of Cayor and Baol where
*   the arms of the baobabs twist in anguish*
All day long, all along the line
Through tiny stations, each exactly like the last,
*   chattering little black girls uncaged from school*
All day long, roughly shaken on the benches of
*   the clanking, dust-covered wheezing antique train*
I come seeking to forget Europe in the pastoral heart of
*   Sine.*

Léopold Sédar Senghor, poet and first president of Senegal.
From "All Day Long"

Day of Association, Senegal

▼▲▼▲▼▲▼▲▼▲▼▲▼

July 15

Copying everyone else all the time, the monkey one day cut his throat.

Zulu of South Africa proverb on conformity. Equivalent to our expression "If everyone jumped off a cliff, would you?"

President's Day, Botswana (July 15–16)

▼▲▼▲▼▲▼▲▼▲▼▲▼

July 16

Merely by describing yourself as black you have started on the road towards emancipation, you have committed yourself to fight against all forces that seek to use your blackness as a stamp that marks you out as a subservient human being.

Steve Biko, South African political activist

▼▲▼▲▼▲▼▲▼▲▼▲▼▲▼

July 17

Throw him into the river and he will rise with a fish in his mouth.

Egyptian expression for an extremely lucky person

▼▲▼▲▼▲▼▲▼▲▼▲▼▲▼

July 18

What a day, when the morning air does not resound with the pounding of yams!
What a day, when I listened in vain to hear them sift the flour!
When the frying pots do not simmer with the fricassee of rabbits and birds.
What a day, when the expert wakes up under the shadow of starvation!

Traditional Yoruba of Nigeria poem

▼▲▼▲▼▲▼▲▼▲▼▲▼▲▼

July 19

The Bini people of West Africa believe that a falling star foretells the death of a prince.

They also believe that it is a bad sign to strike your right foot on something before embarking on a journey.

▼▲▼▲▼▲▼▲▼▲▼▲▼

July 20

As for me if the world turns this way I take it; if it turns another way I take it. Any way the world turns I take it with my hands. I like sleep and my wife and my one son, so I do not think.

Gabriel Okara, Nigerian writer. From *The Voice*, 1964

▼▲▼▲▼▲▼▲▼▲▼▲▼

July 21

The bad neighbor sees only what enters the house, not what goes from it.

Egyptian expression concerning someone who sees only
another person's gains while remaining blind to their
charitable qualities

▼▲▼▲▼▲▼▲▼▲▼▲▼

July 22

The body perishes, the heart stays young,
The platter wears away with the serving of food:
No log retains its bark when old,
No lover peaceful while the rival weeps.

Traditional Swazi and Zulu of southern Africa song about
aging

King's Birthday (Sobhuza II), Swaziland

▼▲▼▲▼▲▼▲▼▲▼▲▼

July 23

The hot-headed man is like a tree in an open field;
In the blast of a moment its leaves are gone,
And it is shipped down to the shipyard.
It is floated far from its native place
Until, at last, the flame becomes its burial shroud.

But the really humble man keeps to himself;
He grows like a tree in the garden,
One that flourishes and doubles its yield.
With sweet fruit and pleasant shade
It stands before its lord,
Until the day it dies in its own grove.

Advice from the "Teaching of Amen-em-opet," an ancient
Egyptian text believed to have been written during the
Nineteenth Dynasty, c. 1200 B.C.

Revolution Day, Egypt

▼▲▼▲▼▲▼▲▼▲▼▲▼

July 24

Ga of Ghana riddle:
  What do you look at with one eye, but never with two?

Answer: The inside of a bottle.

▼▲▼▲▼▲▼▲▼▲▼▲▼

July 25

Respect yourself, you will get it back.

Tunisian proverb

Republic Day, Tunisia

▼▲▼▲▼▲▼▲▼▲▼▲▼

July 26

The house looks good from the outside, but the inside is bad.

Vai of Liberia expression for someone who has an impressive
appearance, but has a bad character

Independence Day, Liberia

▼▲▼▲▼▲▼▲▼▲▼▲▼

July 27

A conversation with a friend and a proverb from an old lady; while
interesting, one must leave them.

Oromo of Ethiopia and Kenya proverb on the temporary nature
of joy

▼▲▼▲▼▲▼▲▼▲▼▲▼

July 28

Between tree and bark it's dangerous to poke your
finger.

Expression warning one not to get involved in the problems of
people who are intimate with each other, such as married
couples. Found in *Perpetua and the Habit of Unhappiness* by
Mongo Beti of Cameroon, 1974

Pipe of the Bamileke of Cameroon

▼▲▼▲▼▲▼▲▼▲▼▲▼

July 29

Treat the person you know equally with the person you do not.... Let men fear you because you offer justice.... This is laid upon you.

Tuthmosis III, ancient Egyptian king. Instructions to his vizier Rekhmire

▼▲▼▲▼▲▼▲▼▲▼▲▼

July 30

Mtu akiona chungu ya wadudu sisimizi ukutani basi atafikiwa na wageni wa ghafula.

If you see a swarm of ants on the wall, it is a sign that unexpected guests will arrive.

Swahili of East Africa superstition

▼▲▼▲▼▲▼▲▼▲▼▲▼

July 31

The best generosity is that which is quick.

Egyptian proverb

▼▲▼▲▼▲▼▲▼▲▼▲▼

August 1

It happens that a trip to hell ends with a glimpse of light and leads, with God's will, to the promised land.

Nicéphore Soglo, president of Benin, November 1994

National Day, Benin
Parents' day, Zaire

Water spirit mask from benin

▼▲▼▲▼▲▼▲▼▲▼▲▼▲▼

August 2

I am she who cuts across the game reserve
That no girl crosses.
I am the boldest of the bold,
outfacer of wizards.
Obstinate perseverer,
The nation swore at me
and ate their words.
She cold shoulders kings and
despises mere commoners.

First verse of Zulu of South Africa women's praise song

▼▲▼▲▼▲▼▲▼▲▼▲▼▲▼

August 3

The poorer you are, the less you get.

Hamani Diori, first president of Niger

Independence Day, Niger
Anniversary of the Killing of Pidjiguiti, Guinea-Bissau

▼▲▼▲▼▲▼▲▼▲▼▲▼▲▼

August 4

Silence is also a form of speech.

Fulani of West Africa proverb

National Day, Burkina Faso

▼▲▼▲▼▲▼▲▼▲▼▲▼

August 5

Spoken words are living things like cocoa-beans packed with life. And like cocoa-beans they grow and give life....They will enter some insides, remain there and grow like the corn blooming on the alluvial soil at the river side.

Gabriel Okara, Nigerian Writer. From *The Voice*, 1964

Farmers' Day, Zambia

▼▲▼▲▼▲▼▲▼▲▼▲▼

August 6

A LEOPARD IN THE BUSH
A Yoruba of Nigeria Folktale

Once a young man went into the bush to go hunting. He saw behind a tree what looked to him like a leopard and quickly ran home to tell his father. The father was so relieved that his son had escaped death that he immediately began to prepare a feast. The young man told his father about his adventure in the forest. As he talked he increased the size of the beast, while his father increased the number of chickens he planned to kill for the feast. The son continued on and on, until he finally mentioned that the animal was eating okra. The father stopped cold: he realized the animal his son had seen was not a leopard—it was a harmless antelope. Extremely vexed, he scolded his braggart son for not killing the antelope for their evening meal.

This folktale gave rise to the Yoruba proverb "Too much talking spoils the leopard in the bush."

▼▲▼▲▼▲▼▲▼▲▼▲▼

August 7

To crawl on one's hands and knees has never prevented one from walking upright.

Meru of Kenya proverb

▼▲▼▲▼▲▼▲▼▲▼▲▼

August 8

A house should not be built so close to another that a chicken from one can lay an egg in the neighbor's yard, nor so far away that a child cannot shout to the yard of his neighbor.

Julius K. Nyerere, first president of Tanzania

Nane Nane (Farmers' Day), Tanzania

▼▲▼▲▼▲▼▲▼▲▼▲▼

August 9

We have seen the future, and it wears skirts.

Bill Krige, South African journalist

National Woman's Day, South Africa
Mouloud (commemorates the birth of the prophet Mohammed), observed in
   Muslim countries and communities across Africa (date varies)

▼▲▼▲▼▲▼▲▼▲▼▲▼

August 10

Naked Woman, black woman
Clothed with your color which is life, with your form which is beauty!
In your shadows I have grown up; the gentleness of your hands was
    laid over my eyes.
And now, high up on the sun-baked pass, at the heart of summer, at the
    heart of noon, I come upon you, my Promised Land.
And your beauty strikes me to the heart like the flash of an eagle.

> Léopold Sédar Senghor, first president of Senegal. First verse
> of "Black Woman"

▼▲▼▲▼▲▼▲▼▲▼▲▼

August 11

Eyes which have met have established relationship.

> Shona of Zimbabwe proverb

Heroes' Day, Zimbabwe
Independence Day, Chad

▼▲▼▲▼▲▼▲▼▲▼▲▼

August 12

"Father," Palmieri said to Le Guen, "dealing with one's superiors
is a hell of a problem, isn't it? I haven't been in this game very long,
but I'm finding it an alarming business already."

"It all depends where you want to end up," Le Guen said,
benevolently. "If you frequently dream of being a Colonial Governor, then you should be watching your step already. Otherwise it's
all as easy as kiss-your-hand. There's one infallible method. . . . If a
storm blows, become a reed—a small, very flexible reed. As soon

as the storm is past, you can stand up straight once more. It's very simple."

Mongo Beti, Cameroonian novelist. From *King Lazarus*, 1958

Defense Forces Day, Zimbabwe

▼▲▼▲▼▲▼▲▼▲▼▲▼

August 13

Better to blush than keep the burden in your heart.

Tunisian saying advising that it is healthier to say or do things that are embarrassing but necessary, than to keep them inside where they will fester

Women's Day, Tunisia
Independence Day, Central African Republic

▼▲▼▲▼▲▼▲▼▲▼▲▼

August 14

Any human enterprise is worth the starting. And to start is half the battle.

Driss Chraibi, Moroccan writer. From *Heirs to the Past*, 1962

Oued Ed-Dahab Day (anniversary of the 1979 annexation), Morocco

▼▲▼▲▼▲▼▲▼▲▼▲▼

August 15

Muronga and Makena nod in bewildered agreement as the priest lists the powers of the Holy Father. They haven't the faintest idea about what the Pope is and where Rome is. They cannot even figure out if this "Pope" is male or female. The pictures Pater Dickman has, show him wearing dresses all the time, as women would, but the priest and *Katekete* speak of him as a man. Maybe the Pope is a she-man, like Shamwaka, the man in the next village, who wears women's clothes and cannot get married, Muronga speculates. But Shamwaka is not the chief. I don't understand how a she-man can be a chief. A she-man could never be a chief, Muronga says to himself. He is tempted to ask the priest. . . . But he remembers that it is this priest who chased one catechist away from the mission when he asked whether Mary, the mother of Jesus Christ, broke the marriage law by sleeping with the Holy Ghost. That would have explained how Mary got pregnant without sleeping with her man, Joseph. The catechist's question made perfect sense to Muronga, but kept the priest in a bad temper all week long.

Joseph Diescho, Namibian novelist. From *Born of the Sun*, 1988

Feast of the Assumption of Saint Mary, observed in many countries
Independence Day, Congo

▼▲▼▲▼▲▼▲▼▲▼▲▼

August 16

When God wills that an event will occur, He sets the causes that will lead to it.

Babikr Bedri, Sudanese scholar. From *Memoirs*, 1969

▼▲▼▲▼▲▼▲▼▲▼▲▼

August 17

We must form a united front against the exploitation of man by man; we must cure ourselves of our complexes by a supranational awareness, a national consciousness. Our ridiculous divisions are profitable only to the great powers, which exploit our weaknesses.

Leon M'ba, first president of Gabon

Independence Day, Gabon

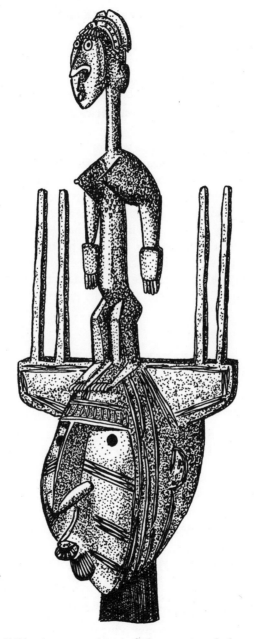

Children's secret society mask from western Sudan

▼▲▼▲▼▲▼▲▼▲▼

August 18

THE TRAVELER AND THE PEANUT FARMER
A Hausa of West Africa Folktale

A man dressed in fancy clothes was on his way to a party. He came across a woman carrying peanuts, who said. "Traveler, let me give you some provisions for your journey." The traveler replied, "One who is about the enjoy the finest delicacies has no use for peanuts," and threw the peanuts she handed him into the mud. As he carried on, he saw that the river had swelled up and there was no way he could make it across. The traveler turned back, biting his fingers. Evening came and he remembered where he had scattered the peanuts. He returned to the site, and had to bend down and pick the peanuts one by one out of the mud for his dinner.

▼▲▼▲▼▲▼▲▼▲▼

August 19

If I had lighted for thee my ten fingers to use as candles thou would still regard them as if they were in darkness.

Egyptian expression for those who are ungrateful and forgetful of favors

▼▲▼▲▼▲▼▲▼▲▼

August 20

One day is in favor of you, and another day against you.

Moroccan proverb commenting on the fickleness of life

The King and People's Revolution, Morocco

▼▲▼▲▼▲▼▲▼▲▼▲▼

August 21

I am convinced that, in the history of the human race, imperialists and racists will also become extinct. They are now very powerful. But they are a very primitive animal. The only difference between them and these other extinct creatures is that their teeth and claws are more elaborate and cause much greater harm....a failure to cooperate together is a mark of bestiality, it is not a characteristic of humanity.

> Julius K. Nyerere, first president of Tanzania. From "All Men Are Created Equal." A speech delivered at Chang'ombe Teacher's College, August 21, 1972

▼▲▼▲▼▲▼▲▼▲▼▲▼

August 22

Biyo socdaa biyo fadhiyo dhagaajiyo.
Flowing water makes stagnant water move.

> Somali proverb

▼▲▼▲▼▲▼▲▼▲▼▲▼

August 23

I had a date in the bush
With all the gods,
So I went.

I had a date in the bush
With all the trees,
So I went.

I had a date in the mountain
*   with the Kontomblé.*
I went because I had to go.

I had to go away to learn
*   How to know.*
I had to go away to learn
*   How to grow.*
I had to go away to learn
*   How to stay here.*

So I went and knocked at doors
*   Locked in front of me.*
*   I craved to enter.*
*   Oh, little did I know*
The doors did not lead outside.

*   It was all in me.*
I was the room and the door.
*   It was all in me.*
I just had to remember.

*   And I learned that I lived*
*   Always and everywhere.*
I learned that I knew everything.
*   Only I had forgotten.*
*   I learned that I grew*
Only I had overlooked things.
Now I am back, remembering.

I want to be what I know I am,
And take the road we always
*   forget to take.*
Because I heard the smell
*   Of the things forgotten*
And my belly was touched.

That's why I had a date with the bush.
That's why I had a date with the hill.
That's why I had a date with the world
Under.
Now, father, I'll take you home.
I am back.

Traditional Dagara of West Africa initiation ceremony song

▼▲▼▲▼▲▼▲▼▲▼▲▼

August 24

The goat is not big in cowtown.

Vai of Liberia proverb on the anonymity of people
in foreign places

Flag Day, Liberia
Umhlanga (Reed Dance Day), Swaziland

▼▲▼▲▼▲▼▲▼▲▼▲▼

August 25

One does not escape fate by running.

Ibo of Nigeria proverb

Mask of the Ibo of Nigeria

▼▲▼▲▼▲▼▲▼▲▼▲▼

August 26

Who knows how we shall fashion a land of peace where black outnumbers white so greatly? Some say that the earth has bounty enough for all, and that more for one does not mean less for another, that the advance of one does not mean the decline of another. They say that poor-paid labour means a poor nation, and that better-paid labour means greater markets and greater scope for industry and manufacture. And others say that this is a danger, for better-paid labour will not only buy more but will also read more, think more, ask more, and will not be content to be forever voiceless and inferior. . . .

Cry, the beloved country, for the unborn child that is the inheritor of our fear. Let him not love the earth too deeply. Let him not laugh too gladly when the water runs through his fingers, nor stand too silent when the setting sun makes red the veld with fire. Let him not be too moved when the birds of his land are singing, nor give too much of his heart to a mountain or valley. For fear will rob him of all if he gives too much.

> Alan Paton, South African writer. From *Cry the Beloved Country*, 1948

Heroes' Day, Namibia

▼▲▼▲▼▲▼▲▼▲▼▲▼

August 27

To take part in the African revolution, it is not enough to write a revolutionary song; you must fashion the revolution with the people. And if you fashion it with the people, the songs will come by themselves.

> Sékou Touré, first president of Guinea, address to the Second Congress of Black Writers and Artists, Rome, Italy, 1959

▼▲▼▲▼▲▼▲▼▲▼▲▼

August 28

He that is not jealous is not in love.

There is no greater invitation to love than loving first.

> Saint Augustine of Hippo (A.D. 354–430). Saint from northern
> Africa (present-day Algeria)

Feast Day for Saint Augustine

▼▲▼▲▼▲▼▲▼▲▼▲▼

August 29

> *I am a small boy*
> *But I am the gentleman of the future;*
> *I am the goodness of my land*
> *And I will do my best;*
> *Teach me that my mind*
> *May accept the word of learning;*
> *Learning is power*
> *Learning is the best.*

> Dinka of southern Sudan song for motivating children to
> attend school

▼▲▼▲▼▲▼▲▼▲▼▲▼

August 30

Mwenye kwenda kulala na kiu usiku, roho yake itakuwa inatangatanga;
paka akiigundua ataivamia na mtu atakufa papo hapo.

If a person goes to bed thirsty, his soul will wander about at night;
if a cat sees it she will pounce on it and the person will die at once.

> Swahili of East Africa superstition

▼▲▼▲▼▲▼▲▼▲▼▲▼▲▼

August 31

When minds are the same, that which is far off will come.

East African proverb

▼▲▼▲▼▲▼▲▼▲▼▲▼

September 1

Ariririrririti!
Step like that father and step again
The terror of the Maasai,
The terror of all our enemy,
You who conquered all the Maasai,
You chased away the nations
that are our enemies with a sword,
Step like that and do it again!

Embu of Kenya song for a brave warrior

Heroes' Day, Tanzania
Anniversary of the Start of the Armed Struggle, Eritrea
Revolution Day, Libya

▼▲▼▲▼▲▼▲▼▲▼▲▼

September 2

Yoruba of Nigeria riddle:
    Who has a house too small for guests?

Answer: A turtle.

Dance mask of the Basonge of Zaire

▼▲▼▲▼▲▼▲▼▲▼▲▼

September 3

Walk five hundred steps in my city, and you change civilizations: here is an Arab town, its houses like expressionless faces, its long, silent, shadowed passages leading suddenly to packed crowds. Then, the busy Jewish alleys, so sordid and familiar, lined with deep stalls, shops and eating houses, all shapeless houses piled as they can fit together. Further on, little Sicily, where abject poverty waits on the doorstep, and then the *fondouks*, the collective tenements of the Maltese, those strange Europeans with an Arab tongue and a British nationality....

And within this great variety, where everyone feels at home but no one feels at ease, each man is shut up in his own neighbour-hood, in fear, hate, and contempt of his neighbor. Like the filth and untidiness of this stinking city, we've known fear and scorn since the first awakening of our consciousness.

Albert Memmi, Tunisian novelist and poet. From *The Pillar of Salt*, 1956. Memmi describes his birthplace, Tunis

Memorial Day, Tunisia

▼▲▼▲▼▲▼▲▼▲▼▲▼

September 4

A day in school will profit you,
For its work endures like the mountains.

Would that I could make you love books,
Even more than your own mother.

From the "Instruction of Duauf," an ancient Egyptian text written during the Eleventh or Twelfth Dynasty, c. 2150–1990 B.C. Duauf, a magistrate, gives advice to his son Pepy

▼▲▼▲▼▲▼▲▼▲▼▲▼

September 5

THE RIVAL STORYTELLERS
A Vai of Liberia Folktale

There were two famous storytellers who lived in the same town. Each had heard of the other. One evening they met at a dinner party. When dinner was finished the first storyteller began talking. He told, among other things, of his travels to a neighboring country where everything was exceptionally big.

He said, "I personally witnessed the passing of a bird so huge that it took seven days for its neck to go by."

The other storyteller sat up in his chair and said, "You know, I believe you are right, because when I was there, I saw a tree so enormous that a team of ten strong men using axes were unable to cut it down, even after trying for six months."

"That is not possible," said the first storyteller. "How could it be that ten strong men couldn't cut a tree down in six months?"

"Well, if this tree didn't exist," asked the second storyteller, "where would your bird have been able to sit down?"

▼▲▼▲▼▲▼▲▼▲▼▲▼

September 6

It is in the nature of man to yearn and struggle for freedom. The germ of freedom is in every individual, in anyone who is a human being. In fact, the history of mankind is the history of man struggling and striving for freedom.

> Chief Albert Luthuli of South Africa, former president of the African National Congress and recipient of the Nobel peace prize

Somhlolo (Independence Day), Swaziland

▼▲▼▲▼▲▼▲▼▲▼▲▼

September 7

In the revolutionary school
I know why I study—
But in the colonial school
I was studying like the blind.

Elisa de Silveira, Mozambican secondary school student, 1978
From Chris Searle's *We're Building a New School, Diary of a*
Teacher in Mozambique, 1981

Victory Day (anniversary of the end of the armed struggle), Mozambique

▼▲▼▲▼▲▼▲▼▲▼▲▼

September 8

Wisdom is the finest beauty of a person.
Money does not prevent you from becoming blind.
Money does not prevent you from becoming mad.
Money does not prevent you from becoming lame.
You may be ill in any part of your body,
So it is better for you to go and think again
And to select wisdom....

Yoruba of Nigeria oracle poem

▼▲▼▲▼▲▼▲▼▲▼▲▼

September 9

Love me as if I were your brother but do your accounts with me as
if I were your enemy.

Tunisian expression warning that one should keep friendship
and business separate in order to preserve friendship

▼▲▼▲▼▲▼▲▼▲▼▲▼

September 10

Just before seven a most sophisticated-looking young woman had driven in and knocked down all our plans. Chief Nanga introduced her as Barrister Mrs. Akilo, and she had come that very minute from another town eighty miles away. She said she hadn't even checked in at the hotel or washed off the dust of the journey. I thought she was beautiful enough with the dust on and I remembered the proverbial joke in my village about a certain woman whose daughter was praised for her beauty and she said: "you haven't see her yet; wait till she's had a bath."

Chinua Achebe, Nigerian writer. From *A Man of the People*, 1966

▼▲▼▲▼▲▼▲▼▲▼▲▼

September 11

When demanded in the name of the Negus, not only the person but the running water stops.

Ethiopian proverb reflecting traditional respect for the King
(called the Negus)

Enkutatash (New Year's Day), Ethiopia

Cross of Gonder, Ethiopia

▼▲▼▲▼▲▼▲▼▲▼▲▼

September 12

Thank you my daughter
who fetches me firewood.
There were two people
who were in seclusion
who won the raid.
Nowadays
there are no raids.
Thank you my son
for winning the raid.
Thank you my daughter
who collects firewood for me.
Nowadays
there are no raids.
Education is the raid
The book is the shield
The pen is the spear
Raid is on ignorance
Raid is on ignorance.

Kalenjin of Kenya children's song

▼▲▼▲▼▲▼▲▼▲▼▲▼

September 13

To be happy in one's home is better than
to be a chief.

Yoruba of Nigeria proverb

Harp of the Mangbetu of Zaire

▼▲▼▲▼▲▼▲▼▲▼▲▼

September 14

Look, the whole world
is moved forward by good character;
when character is not good,
no wonder there is loss.
The most wonderful thing
is a wise character.

Shaaban Roberts, Swahili poet

▼▲▼▲▼▲▼▲▼▲▼▲▼

September 15

Thou kissest thy lover, and tearest out his teeth.

Egyptian proverb on greediness

▼▲▼▲▼▲▼▲▼▲▼▲▼

September 16

Put learning in your heart,
That you may escape the drudgery of hard labor.

Become a man of reputation,
For who can recall the name of the boy who was lazy in school?
Now he is loaded down like an ass,
Like a beast that carries for his master,
The one who knows what he is really worth.

Set your heart on learning,
That you may direct the work of the world.

Advice from "Exhortations," ancient Egyptian texts used to
teach writing in scribal schools

▼▲▼▲▼▲▼▲▼▲▼▲▼

September 17

A train
climbing from a difficult African vale
creaking and creaking slow and absurd

It shrills and shrills...

Many lives
have drenched the land
where the rails lie
crushed under the weight of the engine
and the din of the third class...

Slow absurd and cruel
the African train...

Agostinho Neto, *African Train*

National Heroes' Day (birthday of Agostinho Neto, first president), Angola
Ganesh Chaturthi (Hindu festival), Mauritius

▼▲▼▲▼▲▼▲▼▲▼▲▼

September 18

The lazy one is pregnant during the sowing season.

Burundian proverb

Victory of Union for National Progress (UPRONA) Party, Burundi

▼▲▼▲▼▲▼▲▼▲▼▲▼

September 19

The one who does not love me,
He will become a frog
And he will jump jump away.
And he will become a monkey with one leg
And he will hop hop hop away.

Yoruba of Nigeria children's song

▼▲▼▲▼▲▼▲▼▲▼▲▼

September 20

Ucoka m'ukonde ndi kuleza.

It is patience which gets you out of the net.

Nyanja of Malawi proverb

▼▲▼▲▼▲▼▲▼▲▼▲▼

September 21

Were you to come to our village as a tourist, it is likely, my son, that you would not stay long. If it were wintertime...you would find that a dark cloud had descended over the village. This, my son, would not be dust, nor yet the mist which rises up after rainfall. It would be a swarm of those sandflies which obstruct all paths to those who wish to enter our village....If you were to come to us in summer you would find the horseflies with us—enormous flies the size of young sheep, as we say....And were you to come at a time which was neither summer nor winter you would find nothing at all....We have become used to this hard life, in fact we like it, but we ask no one to subject himself to the difficulties of our life.

Tayeb Salih, Sudanese writer. From "The Doum Tree of Wad Hamid," in *Wedding of Zein and Other Stories*, 1968

▼▲▼▲▼▲▼▲▼▲▼▲▼

September 22

A man of power may be right or wrong, but he is always right.

Bambara of West Africa proverb

Independence Day, Mali

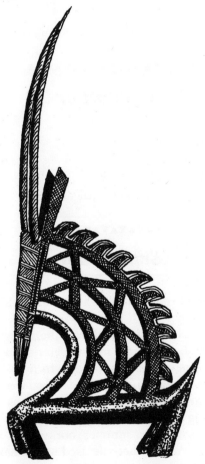

Crown of a headdress of the Bambara of Mali

▼▲▼▲▼▲▼▲▼▲▼▲▼

September 23

Likikuangukia jani la mti moja kwa moja mpaka juu ya kichwa chako ni alama kuwa utavaa kofia mpya.

If a leaf from a tree falls directly onto your head, it is a sign that you will wear a new hat.

▼▲▼▲▼▲▼▲▼▲▼▲▼

September 24

Human beings are perhaps never more frightened than when they are convinced beyond doubt that they are right.

Laurens Van der Post, South African writer and explorer. From *The Lost World of the Kalahari*, 1958

Heritage Day, South Africa
National Day, Guinea-Bissau
Anniversary of Failed Attack on Lomé, Togo

▼▲▼▲▼▲▼▲▼▲▼▲▼

September 25

Pack up for the journey, pack up quickly,
Pack up for the journey, pack up quickly.
Orders—whose orders?
Orders of the Bwana Captain, the Army's orders.

Pack up for the journey, let's go to battle,
Pack up for the journey, let's go to battle.
Let us fight and defeat the enemy,
The enemy are sleeping in their trenches.

When we have beaten the enemy we shall come home,
And the children will be waiting and clapping their hands,
We shall start digging our gardens,
And we shall look after our cattle for the rest of our lives.

A King's African Rifles marching song from the 1960s

Armed Forces Day, Mozambique
Republic Day, Rwanda

▼▲▼▲▼▲▼▲▼▲▼▲▼

September 26

You can live without ever being ill, be as strong as a cedar of the Atlas mountains, yet have been dead for a long time because you've done nothing with your life.

Driss Chraibi, Moroccan writer. From *Heirs to the Past*, 1962

▼▲▼▲▼▲▼▲▼▲▼▲▼

September 27

An old pot makes water sweet and quickly boils.

Oromo of Ethiopia and Kenya proverb in praise of age

Maskal (Finding of the True Cross), Ethiopia, Eritrea

Cross of Gojam, Ethiopia

▼▲▼▲▼▲▼▲▼▲▼▲▼

September 28

Everybody loves a fool, but nobody wants him for a son.

Malinke of West Africa proverb

▼▲▼▲▼▲▼▲▼▲▼▲▼

September 29

"In more civilised countries," said Palmieri, who was a very high-flying sort of humanist, "it is, perhaps, true that people don't half-kill each other anymore for such base motives. But it's not very long since much less than that would have caused a duel, even in Europe. It's Humanity as a whole that refuses to develop as it should. We all have our wretched little individual pride some-where. In the Middle Ages it called itself chivalry. Later it disguised itself as a sense of honour. In our day dignity is all the rage."

Mongo Beti, Cameroonian novelist. From *King Lazarus*, 1958

▼▲▼▲▼▲▼▲▼▲▼▲▼

September 30

Go the way that many people go; if you go alone you will have reason to lament.

Lozi of Botswana and Zambia proverb

Botswana Day, Botswana (September 30–October 1)

▼▲▼▲▼▲▼▲▼▲▼▲▼

October 1

In the beginning God created the universe. Then he created the moon, the stars and the wild beasts of the forests. On the sixth day he created the Nigerian. But on the seventh day while God rested, the Nigerian invented noise.

Anthony Enahoro, *How to Be a Nigerian*, 1966

Blessed are the common people. God loves them: that is why he made millions of them.

Nnamdi Azikiwe, first president of Nigeria, 1948

National Day, Nigeria

▼▲▼▲▼▲▼▲▼▲▼▲▼

October 2

Now, there is no dignity without freedom. We prefer poverty in liberty to riches in slavery.

Sékou Touré, first president of Guinea. From a letter to General de Gaulle of France, 1958

Independence Day, Guinea

Rice harvest mask of the Baga of Guinea

▼▲▼▲▼▲▼▲▼▲▼▲▼

October 3

An Embu and Kalenjin of Kenya riddle:
   What containers hang upside down but their contents do not
   pour out?

Answer: An animal's udders.

▼▲▼▲▼▲▼▲▼▲▼▲▼

October 4

He seemed perfectly calm as he sat down, but his heart was
thumping wildly. Two conflicting ideas now seeped through him.
The one said, "You have no right to sit on the bench." The other
questioned, "Why have you no right to sit on the bench?" The first
spoke of the past, of the life on the farm, of the servile figure of his
father and Ou Klaas, his father's father who had said, "God in his
wisdom made the white man white and black man black." The
other voice had promise of the future in it and said, "Karlie, you
are a man. You have dared what your father would not have dared.
And his father. You will die like a man."
   Karlie took out a Cavalla from the crumpled packet and
smoked. But nobody seemed to notice him sitting there. . . . The
world still pursued its natural way. People still lived, breathed and
laughed. No voice shouted triumphantly, "Karlie, you have conquered!" He was a perfectly ordinary human being sitting on a
bench on a crowded station, smoking a cigarette. Or was this his
victory? Being an ordinary human being sitting on a bench?

   Richard Rive, South African writer. From *The Bench*, 1983

Independence Day, Lesotho

Spirit mask from Gabon

▼▲▼▲▼▲▼▲▼▲▼▲▼

October 5

Little and lasting is better than much and passing.

Moroccan proverb

▼▲▼▲▼▲▼▲▼▲▼▲▼

October 6

Be skillful in the speaker's art,
For there is power in the tongue,
And good speech prevails over fighting.

Advice from the "Instruction of King Merikare," an ancient
Egyptian text written during the Eighteenth Dynasty
(1570–c. 1342 B.C.)

Armed Forces Day, Egypt

▼▲▼▲▼▲▼▲▼▲▼▲▼

October 7

Thou knowest that I sit waiting for the moon to turn back, that I may listen to all the people's stories....For I am here—in a great city—I do not obtain stories....I do merely listen, watching for a story which I want to hear; that it may float into my ear....I will go to sit at my home that I may listen, turn my ears backwards to the heels of my feet on which I wait, so that I can feel that a story is in the wind.

> Statement of a Bushman held prisoner in the late 1800s
> in South Africa

National Sports Day, Lesotho
Evacuation Day, Libya

▼▲▼▲▼▲▼▲▼▲▼▲▼

October 8

Tell little, little lies—as tiny as needles. When they get as big as a hoe, they will strike you dead.

> Yoruba of Nigeria proverb

▼▲▼▲▼▲▼▲▼▲▼▲▼

October 9

A mother lying down sees farther than a child in a tree.

> Krio of Sierra Leone proverb

A mother's tears are no hard work.

> Mongo of Zaire proverb meaning that a mother's love doesn't
> know fatigue

Mother's Day, Malawi (second Monday in October)
Independence Day, Uganda

I khoko pendant of the Bapende of Zaire

▼▲▼▲▼▲▼▲▼▲▼▲▼

October 10

Search in your past for what is good and beautiful. Build your future from there.

Paul Kruger, (1825–1904) South African statesman

Kruger Day, South Africa

▼▲▼▲▼▲▼▲▼▲▼▲▼

October 11

The Turkana of Kenya believe that if an owl lands on someone's house misfortune will come to that house: someone is likely to become sick or even die. There are two ways to avert the disaster. If the family has animals, it must kill a goat of the same color as the owl. If the family doesn't have animals, it must make a clay model of the owl and place it on the spot where the owl landed. A string must them be tied around the clay owl's neck, and everyone in the family must pull it toward the west. Then the house will be left in peace.

▼▲▼▲▼▲▼▲▼▲▼▲▼

October 12

Nobody can use another person's teeth to smile.

> Kalenjin of Kenya proverb advising to take care of one's own business

▼▲▼▲▼▲▼▲▼▲▼▲▼

October 13

THE HARE AND THE LION
An Ethiopian Fable
by Lokman (c. 1100 B.C.)

A hare upon meeting a lioness one day said reproachfully, "I have always a great number of children, while you have only one or two now and then." The lioness replied, "That is true, but my one child is a lion."

▼▲▼▲▼▲▼▲▼▲▼▲▼

October 14

A kind person is the one who is kind to strangers.

> Bakongo of Zaire proverb

President Mobutu's Birthday and Youth Day, Zaire

Neckrest of the Luba of Zaire

▼▲▼▲▼▲▼▲▼▲▼▲▼

October 15

A living dog is better than a dead lion.

Tunisian proverb

Evacuation Day, Tunisia
Anniversary of the 1987 Coup, Burkina Faso

▼▲▼▲▼▲▼▲▼▲▼▲▼

October 16

If a poor man is found to owe you a great debt,
*   divide it three ways;*
remit two parts and let the third stand.
That, you will see, is the best way in this life;
thereafter you will sleep sound and in the morning

it will seem like good tidings;
for it is better to be praised for neighborly love
than to have riches in your store room;
better to enjoy your bread with good conscience
than to have wealth weighed down by reproaches.

Advice from "Teaching of Amen-em-opet," an ancient Egyptian
text believed to have been written during the Nineteenth
Dynasty (c. 1342–1200 B.C.)

▼▲▼▲▼▲▼▲▼▲▼▲▼

October 17

Yoruba of Nigeria riddle:
When does a man run through thornbushes?

Answer: When something is chasing him.

▼▲▼▲▼▲▼▲▼▲▼▲▼

October 18

BAOBAB TREES

An African Legend

It is believed that when God first created baobab trees, they
refused to stay rooted and walked around the earth. So, God
replanted them upside down, which explains why they look like
their roots are up in the air.

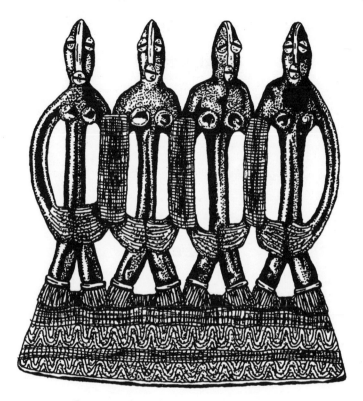

Bronze pendant of the Senufo of Côte d'Ivoire

▼▲▼▲▼▲▼▲▼▲▼▲▼

October 19

The head in the heavens, the hinder parts in water.

Egyptian expression for those who put on airs undeservedly

▼▲▼▲▼▲▼▲▼▲▼▲▼

October 20

Our children may learn about heroes of the past. Our task is to make ourselves architects of the future.

Jomo Kenyatta, first president of Kenya

Kenyatta Day (anniversary of the death of the first president), Kenya

▼▲▼▲▼▲▼▲▼▲▼▲▼

October 21

Ni nuksi kufanya neno lako kwa mara ya awali siku ya mwezi ishirini na moja.

It is unlucky to do anything for the first time on the twenty-first of the month.

Swahili of East Africa superstition

▼▲▼▲▼▲▼▲▼▲▼▲▼

October 22

Mwana ndi bango akafa apuka wina.

When a man or a reed dies another springs up.

Nyanja of Malawi proverb on replaceability, used particularly when a person dies or leaves a spouse

Cross of Dese, Ethiopia

▼▲▼▲▼▲▼▲▼▲▼▲▼

October 23

If one is not in a hurry, even an egg will start walking.

Ethiopian proverb

▼▲▼▲▼▲▼▲▼▲▼▲▼

October 24

Some people draw a comforting distinction between "force" and "violence." . . . I refuse to cloud the issue by such word-play. . . . The power which establishes a state is violence; the power which maintains it is violence; the power which eventually overthrows it is violence. . . . Call an elephant a rabbit only if it gives you comfort to feel that you are about to be trampled to death by a rabbit.

Kenneth Kaunda, first president of Zambia. From *Kaunda on Violence*, 1980

Independence Day, Zambia
United Nations Day, Swaziland

▼▲▼▲▼▲▼▲▼▲▼▲▼

October 25

Obanije mba ara re je.

One who damages the character of another damages his own.

Yoruba of Nigeria proverb

▼▲▼▲▼▲▼▲▼▲▼▲▼

October 26

You can outdistance that which is running after you but not what is running inside you.

Rwandan proverb. Found in *The Dark Romance of Dian Fossey* by
Harold Hayes, 1991

In a court of fowls, a cockroach never wins his case.

Rwandan proverb

Armed Forces Day, Rwanda

▼▲▼▲▼▲▼▲▼▲▼▲▼

October 27

I no longer have a borrowed soul. I no longer have borrowed thoughts or ideas. I no longer speak in a borrowed language.

Mobutu Sese Seko, first president of Zaire. Quoted in the *San
Francisco Examiner and Chronicle,* June 25, 1972. Seko explains
why his country changed its name from the Democratic
Republic of the Congo to Zaire

Anniversary of the Country's Name Change, Zaire

▼▲▼▲▼▲▼▲▼▲▼▲▼

October 28

Generations pass away and others stand in their place
  Since the time of them that were old....
Rejoice, and let thy heart forget that day when they shall
  lay thee to rest.
Cast all sorrow behind thee, and bethink thee of joy
  until there comes that day of reaching port in the
  land that loveth silence.... Lo, none
  may take his goods with him, and none that hath
  gone may come again.

"Song of the Harper," ancient Egyptian text, written during
the Twelfth Dynasty, c. 1850 B.C.

Dance mask of the Chokwe of Angola, Zaire, and Zambia

▼▲▼▲▼▲▼▲▼▲▼▲▼

October 29

When a fool shakes his rattle, it should always be another fool who dances.

Ahmadou Kourouma, Ivorian writer. From *The Suns of Independence*. 1968

▼▲▼▲▼▲▼▲▼▲▼▲▼

October 30

The mystic drum beat in my inside
and fishes danced in the rivers
and men and women danced on land
to the rhythm of my drum

But standing behind a tree
with leaves around her waist
she only smiled with a shake of her head.

Gabriel Okara, Nigerian writer. From "The Mystic Drum."

▼▲▼▲▼▲▼▲▼▲▼▲▼

October 31

God bless him who pays visits, and short visits.

Egyptian proverb

▼▲▼▲▼▲▼▲▼▲▼▲▼

November 1

She leaned forward, laughed, took a corner of her haïk and tied it to her waist; then she asked the young man to hold the other end. She turned slowly, barely moving her feet, until she was entirely wrapped in it. "Thank you," she said. "May God guide you on the right path! You have beautiful eyes. Get rid of that moustache. Virility lies not in the body, but in the soul. Farewell, I have other books to open."

She looked at me, suddenly motionless, and said:

"Where are you from, you who never speak?

She left without waiting for an answer.

I would have liked to tell her of my life. She would have made it a book to carry from village to village. I can see her opening the chapters of my story one by one, keeping the final secret to herself.

Tahar Ben Jelloun, Moroccan poet and novelist. From *The Sacred Night*, 1989

Anniversary of the Revolution, Algeria
All Saints' Day, observed in many countries

▼▲▼▲▼▲▼▲▼▲▼▲▼

November 2

Swahili of East Africa riddle:

What things always chase each other but never overtake one another?

Answer: The wheels of a vehicle.

▼▲▼▲▼▲▼▲▼▲▼▲▼

November 3

It is said that one cannot pierce the sky to get rain for one's garden.
Nor can one drive the farm, as one drives animals, to the place where
*   rain is falling.*
Worst of all, one cannot abandon one's farm, even though barren,
*   because all one's efforts are invested in it.*
The farmer, in counter argument, replies:
A man with no fixed place in this world cannot claim one in heaven.

Somali poem comparing a nomadic-pastoral life to the
sedentary life of farming.

▼▲▼▲▼▲▼▲▼▲▼▲▼

November 4

Do not call a person a witch before he has bewitched you.

Kalenjin of Kenya proverb warning not to blindly accept the
harmful beliefs of others, but to draw one's own conclusions

Snake bracelet of the Rendille of Kenya

▼▲▼▲▼▲▼▲▼▲▼▲▼

November 5

She brought out her copy of the African Encyclopedia, the pride of her little library, and read through the entries on these names. In no case was marriage mentioned. Then a thought struck her: these famous people were all men. What about famous women? Were they judged by their marriage? She scanned through her knowledge of history. Where were the famous women? Aha, there was Florence Nightingale. Who ever heard of her husband? Her lamp was certainly of more interest to historians than her marital status. How about Joan of Arc. Was she married? Her history books did not say so. Queen Amina of Zaria? She probably was married, but no one bothered about her husband. She looked her up. She was right. There was no mention of her marriage. Psch! Why all the fuss? Marriage was good but it was not everything. She could still make a success of her life in spite of her marital failures. Not that she would ever be a Florence Nightingale or Queen Amina...but she certainly could make a small contribution to society.

Elechi Amadi, Nigerian writer. From *Estrangement*, 1986

▼▲▼▲▼▲▼▲▼▲▼▲▼

November 6

Among the walnuts only the empty one speaks.

Moroccan proverb on false arrogance

Anniversary of the Green March, Morocco
Thanksgiving Day, Liberia

▼▲▼▲▼▲▼▲▼▲▼▲▼

November 7

Because he has so many trades, he is unemployed.

> Tunisian expression for those who know a little about
> everything, but do nothing expertly

New Era Day, Tunisia

▼▲▼▲▼▲▼▲▼▲▼▲▼

November 8

WANJIRU THE BEAUTY OF THE HILLS
A Kikuyu of Kenya Folktale

There once was a young woman named Wanjiru. She was the most beautiful of all the nine hills. When she smiled with her milk-white teeth men stopped to admire her. Her sweet laughter echoed across the hills and lured scores of young men to ask for her hand in marriage. But beautiful Wanjiru refused these proposals, claiming that none of the young men were handsome enough.

One day an exceptionally handsome young man came to court Wanjiru. She fell in love at first sight and was quick to accept his marriage proposal. Her parents were also impressed and readily consented to the marriage. The young man paid the dowry and took his new bride away. When the couple arrived at the groom's village, Wanjiru saw that it was filled with people, but none of them were singing or dancing in celebration of her arrival. As they came closer, Wanjiru realized these were not people at all, but ogres. She had been tricked. "I am in great trouble," she said to herself. "Unless I think quickly, these ogres will surely eat me." Her husband asked her to wait inside the hut he had prepared for her. Wanjiru explained that in her village it was customary for the bride to wait outside the hut on a stool. When her husband turned to find a stool, Wanjiru darted toward the path they had followed from her home. Her husband chased her, singing:

"Beautiful Wanjiru, beautiful Wanjiru, where did you go now? Come back. I will not eat you, today...tomorrow I shall eat you."

Wanjiru replied loud and long:

"People of the nine hills, who sold me to an ogre, an ogre that will eat me. My own father, who sold me to an ogre, an ogre that will eat me. Listen to the ogre sing!"

She climbed to the top of the tallest tree she could find. The ogre stood at the foot of the tree continuing his song, while Wanjiru sang ever more feverishly. Wanjiru's brother, who had been hunting in the woods, heard his sister's singing. He snuck up behind the ogre and speared him in the back. "Come down," he called to his sister, "and let us go home." The brother was very angry that his sister had been sold in his absence. Meanwhile, the villagers laughed at pretty Wanjiru. She would even marry a hyena, if he was handsome enough.

▼▲▼▲▼▲▼▲▼▲▼▲▼

November 9

May my outer head not spoil my inner head.

Yoruba of Nigeria proverb

▼▲▼▲▼▲▼▲▼▲▼▲▼

November 10

They say...it's us poor people's riches. You got no food in your guts, and you got no food for your children, but you're rich with them.

Alex La Guma, South African author. From *A Walk in the Night*, 1967

Divali (Hindu festival of lights), Mauritius

▼▲▼▲▼▲▼▲▼▲▼▲▼

November 11

The question in the air
on the shore
on the tongue of everyone
          —Luanda, where are you?

Silence in the streets
Silence on the tongues
Silence in the eyes

—Hey
sister Rose the fishwife
can you tell?

—Brother
I can't tell
have to sell
rush around the city
if you want to eat!

"Lu-u-nch, choose your lu-u-u-nch
sprats or mackerel
fine fish, fine fi-i-i-sh"

Luandino Vieira, Angolan poet. From "Song for Luanda"

Independence Day, Angola
Nso Cultural Week, Kumbo, Cameroon (features wild-horse races through the
  town's streets)

▼▲▼▲▼▲▼▲▼▲▼▲▼

November 12

The midwife can't take the baby for her pay.

> Vai of Liberia expression for unrealistic requests for compensation

National Memorial Day, Liberia

▼▲▼▲▼▲▼▲▼▲▼▲▼

November 13

He who fills his head with other people's words will find no place where he may put his own.

> Moroccan proverb warning against giving undue weight to the counsel of others.

▼▲▼▲▼▲▼▲▼▲▼▲▼

November 14

> *Sun, sweat, greenness and sea,*
> *Centuries of pain and hope;*
> *This is the land of our ancestors.*
> *Fruit of our hands,*
> *Of the flower of our blood:*
> *This is our beloved country.*

Dagger of the Mangbeth of Zaire

(Chorus)
Long live our glorious country!
The banner of our struggle
Has fluttered in the skies.
Forward, against the foreign yoke!
We are going to build
Peace and progress
In our immortal country!

Branches of the same trunk,
Eyes in the same light;
This is the force of our unity!
The sea and the land,
The dawn and the sun are singing
That our struggle has born fruit!

From the national anthem of Guinea-Bissau

Anniversary of the Movement of Readjustment, Guinea-Bissau

▼▲▼▲▼▲▼▲▼▲▼▲▼

November 15

God knows how to find the oppressor,
And he will repay his transgressions with blood.

Trust not that time will forget you,
For judgment regards a lifetime like an hour.

A man's reputation remains after death,
When his deeds will be heaped up around him.

Judgment is eternal;
Only a fool ignores it!

Advice from the "Instruction of King Merikare," an ancient
Egyptian text written during the Eighteenth Dynasty (1570–c.
1342 B.C.)

▼▲▼▲▼▲▼▲▼▲▼▲▼

November 16

A stone thrown in anger never kills a bird.

Yoruba of Nigeria proverb

▼▲▼▲▼▲▼▲▼▲▼▲▼

November 17

We shall soldier no more,
We shall leave it, this army job.
We shall soldier no more,
We shall leave it, this army job.
We shall leave
This army job.
We shall leave
This army job.
We shall leave
Is soldiering ever a good job?

Twi of Ghana soldiers' song from the 1960s

Armed Forces Day, Zaire

▼▲▼▲▼▲▼▲▼▲▼▲▼

November 18

When a thing becomes perfect it soon fades.

Moroccan proverb

Independence Day, Morocco

▼▲▼▲▼▲▼▲▼▲▼▲▼

November 19

Salt comes from the north, gold from the south, but the word of God and the treasures of wisdom are to be found only in Timbuctoo.

> Fifteenth-century Malian proverb. From *The White Monk of Timbuctoo*, 1934

For some people, when you say "Timbuktu" it is like the end of the world, but this is not true. I am from Timbuktu, and I can tell you we are right at the heart of the world.

> Ali Farka Toure, Malian musician

Anniversary of the 1968 Coup, Mali

Ring of the Dogon of Mali

▼▲▼▲▼▲▼▲▼▲▼▲▼

November 20

He gets his passage for nothing, and winks to the wife of the captain of the ship.

Egyptian expression for ingratitude

▼▲▼▲▼▲▼▲▼▲▼▲▼

November 21

It was stormy windy that night
The candle flickering,
Wavering,
Softening the concrete we sat on
For we had no other wealth
But each other's warmth
That night round the candle-light
For our unfried beans and posho.
You remember?

We sat.
You, me, children
We sat.
Our shadows merging into One
A Oneness like
The candle-light!:
Flame
Wick
Wax

Grace Birabwa Isharaza, Ugandan poet. From "Candle-light"

▼▲▼▲▼▲▼▲▼▲▼▲▼

November 22

He who tells the truth is not well liked.

Bambara of West Africa proverb

▼▲▼▲▼▲▼▲▼▲▼▲▼

November 23

Akoseba ti nje odidi odun.

He who waits for a chance may wait for a long time.

Eyes that have beheld the ocean can no longer be afraid of the lagoon.

Yoruba of Nigeria proverbs

▼▲▼▲▼▲▼▲▼▲▼▲▼

November 24

We have long suffered and today we want to breathe the air of freedom. The Creator has given us this share of the earth that goes by the name of the African continent; it belongs to us and we are its only master. It is right to make this continent a continent of justice, law and peace.

Patrice Lumumba, nationalist leader of the Belgian Congo
(now Zaire)

Anniversary of the Second Republic, Zaire

▼▲▼▲▼▲▼▲▼▲▼▲▼

November 25

Mwenye kula mguu ya kuku atakuwa daima katika mwendo tu.

One who eats fowls' legs will become a perpetual wanderer.

Swahili of East Africa superstition

Swahili earring from Paté Island in Kenya

▼▲▼▲▼▲▼▲▼▲▼▲▼

November 26

FROGS IN THE CALABASH
A Hausa of West Africa Fable

Two frogs fell into a calabash filled wth milk and were unable to get out. The frogs were treading milk when one said to the other, "I am getting tired. Today is my last day on Earth." He gave up, sank, and died. The other was also tired, but kept on treading. After some time, his movements turned the oil in the milk into butter and he climbed atop the pat and jumped out.

God has said, "Stand up that I may help you!"

▼▲▼▲▼▲▼▲▼▲▼▲▼

November 27

People are like plants in the wind: they bow down and rise up again.

Malagasy proverb on resilience

Anniversary of President Abdallah's Assassination, Comoros

▼▲▼▲▼▲▼▲▼▲▼▲▼

November 28

Instruction in youth is like engraving in stones.

Berber of North Africa proverb

National Day, Mauritania
Anniversary of the Proclamation of the Republic, Chad

▼▲▼▲▼▲▼▲▼▲▼▲▼▲▼

November 29

As Africans, we face grim imperatives. Africa is not a world unto itself but an integral part of one world. We have to make a new Africa in which all races of men live and work together in the great task of reconstruction.

William V. S. Tubman, sixth president of Liberia

President Tubman's Birthday, Liberia

▼▲▼▲▼▲▼▲▼▲▼▲▼▲▼

November 30

If the state is going to fall it is from the belly.

Akan of Ghana proverb meaning people, like countries, fail because of their own weaknesses

▼▲▼▲▼▲▼▲▼▲▼▲▼

December 1

Our land is uncommonly rich and fruitful, and produces all kinds of vegetables in great abundance. We have plants of Italian corn, and vast quantities of cotton and tobacco. We have spices of various kinds, particularly pepper; and a variety of delicious fruits, together with gums and honey in great abundance. All our work is to improve these blessings of nature. Agriculture is our chief employment; and everyone, even the women and children, are engaged in it. The benefits of such a way of living are felt by us in the general healthiness of the people, and in their vigour and strength.

> Oldanah Equiano of West Africa. From *The Interesting Narrative of the Life of Oldanah Equiano or Gustavas Vassa, the African, Written By Himself,* 1789.

National Farmers' Day, Ghana
National Day, Central African Republic
Democracy Day, Chad

▼▲▼▲▼▲▼▲▼▲▼▲▼

December 2

The only hard thing, rather one of the two hard things, is knowing your purpose in this world. The other which is harder, is not to corrupt it after knowing what your purpose is.

> Gabriel Okara, Nigerian writer. From *The Voice,* 1964

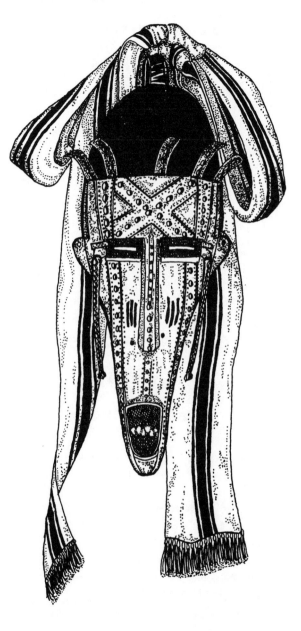

Bronze mask of the Marka of Mali

▼▲▼▲▼▲▼▲▼▲▼▲▼

December 3

Too many captains sink the ship.

> Tunisian expression equivalent to "Too many cooks spoil the broth"

▼▲▼▲▼▲▼▲▼▲▼▲▼

December 4

> *Come here my beloved,*
> *Come, give me a kiss.*
> *There is a new law*
> *which says we must embrace each other.*

> Zulu of South Africa love poem

▼▲▼▲▼▲▼▲▼▲▼▲▼

December 5

At home in South Africa I have sometimes said in big meetings where you have black and white together: "Raise your hands!" Then I've said, "Move your hands," and I've said, "Look at your hands—different colors representing different people. You are the rainbow people of God."

And you remember the rainbow in the Bible is the sign of peace. The rainbow is the sign of prosperity. We want peace, prosperity and justice and we can have it when all the people of God, the rainbow people of God, work together.

> Archbishop Desmond Tutu of South Africa, sermon delivered in Norway, December 5, 1991

▼▲▼▲▼▲▼▲▼▲▼▲▼

December 6

He walks upon the highest part of the wall and says, "For safety
we trust in God!"

Egyptian expression for those who foolishly run in the face of
danger

Mythological god of ancient Egypt

▼▲▼▲▼▲▼▲▼▲▼▲▼

December 7

The streets had no gutters, because there again Independence had played false, they never dug the gutters they promised and they never will; water will swamp the streets as always, and colonized or independent, the African will keep on wading through them until such times as God unpeels the curse stuck fast in their black backsides.

Ahmadou Kourouma, Ivorian writer. From *The Suns of Independence*, 1968

Independence Day, Côte d'Ivoire

▼▲▼▲▼▲▼▲▼▲▼▲▼

December 8

Swahili of East Africa riddle:
I came across a long chain on the road but I could not pick it up. What is it?

Answer: Safari ants.

Immaculate Conception, Seychelles

▼▲▼▲▼▲▼▲▼▲▼▲▼

December 9

In Tanzania it was more than one hundred tribal units which lost their freedom; it was one nation that regained it.

Julius K. Nyerere, first president of Tanzania. From a speech delivered at the University of Toronto, Canada, October 2, 1969

Freedom to many means immediate betterments, as if by magic.... Unless I can meet at least some of these aspirations, my support will wane and my head will roll just as surely as the tickbird follows the rhino.

Nyerere, quoted in *Time* magazine, April 9, 1964

Independence Day, Tanzania

▼▲▼▲▼▲▼▲▼▲▼▲▼

December 10

Poverty makes a free man become a slave.

Twi of Ghana proverb

Human Rights Day, Equatorial Guinea, Namibia

▼▲▼▲▼▲▼▲▼▲▼▲▼

December 11

When the music changes, so should the dance.

Hausa of West Africa proverb on manners

Proclamation of the Republic, Burkina Faso

▼▲▼▲▼▲▼▲▼▲▼▲▼

December 12

Many people may think that, now there is Uhuru [freedom], now I can see the sun of freedom shining, richness will pour down like manna from heaven. I tell you there will be nothing from heaven.

We must all work hard, with our hands, to save ourselves from poverty, ignorance, and disease.

> Jomo Kenyatta, first president of Kenya

Jamhuri (Independence Day), Kenya

▼▲▼▲▼▲▼▲▼▲▼▲▼

December 13

The man who says he will not marry a woman who has other admirers will not marry a woman.

> Yoruba of Nigeria proverb

▼▲▼▲▼▲▼▲▼▲▼▲▼

December 14

Increase your happy times, letting yourself go;
Follow your desire and best advantage.
And "do your thing" while you are still on this earth,
According to the command of your heart.

> "Song of Antuf." Inscribed on the wall of an ancient Egyptian tomb during the Eighteenth Dynasty, c. 1300 B.C.

▼▲▼▲▼▲▼▲▼▲▼▲▼

December 15

Don't laugh at a distant boat being tossed by the waves. Your relatives may be in it.

> Luhya of Kenya proverb warning against delighting in the misfortune of others

▼▲▼▲▼▲▼▲▼▲▼▲▼

December 16

It...surprises me that I could go into a riot in a squatter camp without anybody threatening me or being hostile toward me. I don't understand it. I think that there is something very, very special about black people in this country. People are prepared to listen to me and to judge me as a human being and not merely as someone with a white skin. It amazes me every time I experience it because I don't think that I would have that tolerance if I were in that position.

Hettie V., an Afrikaner journalist and activist

Day of Reconciliation, South Africa

▼▲▼▲▼▲▼▲▼▲▼▲▼

December 17

However long the night may last, there will be morning.

Moroccan proverb used to comfort someone experiencing difficulties

Daylight follows a dark night.

Maasai of Kenya proverb of the same meaning

▼▲▼▲▼▲▼▲▼▲▼▲▼

December 18

A floating log never becomes a crocodile.

Songhai of Niger proverb

Republic Day, Niger

▼▲▼▲▼▲▼▲▼▲▼▲▼

December 19

Fortitude

Like a she-camel with a large bell
Come from the plateau and upper Haud,
My heat is great.

Birds perched together on the same tree
Call each their own cries,
Every country has its own ways,
Indeed people do not understand each other's talk.

One of my she-camels falls on the road
And I protect its meat,
At night I cannot sleep,
And in the daytime I can find no shade.

I have broken my nose on a stick,
I have broken my right hip,
I have something in my eye,
And yet I go on.

Anonymous Somali poem

▼▲▼▲▼▲▼▲▼▲▼▲▼

December 20

The wise with a wink, the fool with a kick.

Egyptian expression about how people are made to understand
things

▼▲▼▲▼▲▼▲▼▲▼▲▼

December 21

The West is on the point of being able to do without man in the production of work....At the same time that work gets along without human life, at that same time it ceases to make human life its final aim; it ceases to value man. Man has never been so unhappy as at this moment when he is accumulating so much.

> Cheikh Hamidou Kane, Senegalese writer. From *Ambiguous Adventure*, 1962

National Tree Planting Day, Malawi

▼▲▼▲▼▲▼▲▼▲▼▲▼

December 22

If you wait for tomorrow, tomorrow comes. If you don't wait for tomorrow, tomorrow comes.

> Malinke of West Africa proverb

▼▲▼▲▼▲▼▲▼▲▼▲▼

December 23

Misfortune is sometimes just good fortune well wrapped up; when the wrapping wears away, good fortune tumbles out.

> Ahmadou Kourouma, Ivorian writer. From *The Suns of Independence*, 1968

Ceremonial mask from Côte d'Ivoire

▼▲▼▲▼▲▼▲▼▲▼▲▼

December 24

Our house is right on the bank of the Nile, so that when I'm lying on my bed at night I put my hand out of the window and idly play with the Nile waters until sleep overtakes me.

Tayeb Salih, Sudanese writer. From *Season of Migration*, 1976

▼▲▼▲▼▲▼▲▼▲▼▲▼

December 25

I have no intention of being an indifferent on-looker if the distant powers have the idea of dividing up Africa, for Ethiopia has been for more than fourteen centuries an island of Christians in the middle of a sea of pagans.

Menelik II, emperor of Ethiopia

Christmas, celebrated throughout Africa
Family Day, Angola

▼▲▼▲▼▲▼▲▼▲▼▲▼

December 26

I thank you God for creating me black.
White is the colour for special occasions
Black is the colour for every day
And I have carried the World since the dawn of time.
And my laugh over the World, through the night,
  creates the day.

Bernard Dadié, Ivorian writer. From "I Thank You God"

Boxing Day, observed in many countries
Family Day, observed in many countries
Day of Goodwill, South Africa

▼▲▼▲▼▲▼▲▼▲▼▲▼

December 27

Bi omode ni aso to baba re, o ni akisa to o?

Just because a child has as many clothes as his father, doesn't mean he has worn out as many clothes as his father.

Yoruba of Nigeria proverb encouraging respect for elders

▼▲▼▲▼▲▼▲▼▲▼▲▼

December 28

Akivua mtu viatu na akaviona kuwa vimepandana inambashiria mtu huyo safari ya ghafula.

When a person takes off a pair of shoes, if one shoe lands on top of the other, that person will set out on an unexpected journey.

Swahili of East Africa belief

▼▲▼▲▼▲▼▲▼▲▼▲▼

December 29

Nin kuu tigay kuma dilin.

He who has warned you has not killed you yet.

Nin ani yiri dad iska sooc.

He who has said "I" has distinguished himself from others.

Somali proverbs

Wooden spoon from Somalia

▼▲▼▲▼▲▼▲▼▲▼▲▼

December 30

What invisible rat
comes from the walls of the night
gnaws at the milky cake of the moon?

Jean-Joseph Rabearivelo, Malagasy poet

Republic Day, Madagascar

▼▲▼▲▼▲▼▲▼▲▼▲▼

December 31

Do what is right all the days of your life;
Comfort the one who weeps;
Do nothing to oppress the widow;
Rob no man of the inheritance of his father;
Respect the authority of the magistrates.

Advice from the "Instruction of King Merikare," an ancient
Egyptian text written during the Eighteenth Dynasty (1570–c.
1342 B.C.)

Revolution Day, Ghana

Sources

CITATIONS

Excerpts from ancient Egyptian texts are from *Ancient Egyptian Proverbs: Selections From the Instructions, Admonitions, and Exhortations of Wise Men and Teachers (2500–1000 B.C.)* by Raymond A. McCoy; *Life of the Ancient Egyptians* by Eugen Strouhal; and *The Mystery of the Pyramids*, by Humphrey Evans.

Swahili love poems and songs are from *A Choice of Flowers: Chaguo la Maua, An Anthology of Swahili Love Poetry*, ed. and trans. Jan Knappert.

Riddles are from *Ji-Nongo-Nongo Means Riddles* by Verna Aardema; *Swahili Sayings*, by S.S. Farsi; *The Living History of Embu and Mbeere* by H. S. K. Mwaniki. "The Clever Bride" is from *Netsebrag*, an Eritrean newsletter published in America.

Many of the political quotations are from *A Political Dictionary of Black Quotations* by Osei Amoah.

Tunisian proverbs are from *1,001 Proverbs From Tunisia* by Isaac Yetiv.

Moroccan proverbs are from *Wit and Wisdom in Morocco* by Edward Westermarck.

Dinka songs are from *The Dinka of the Sudan* by Francis Mading Deng.

Fables and folktales: the South African fable "Why Dogs Sniff at One Another's Tails" is from *Cameos From the Kraal* by M. W. Waters; "Wanjiru the Beauty of the Hills" is adapted from the version recounted by Rose Mwangi in *Kikuyu Folktales*; Goha's tale can be found in *Funk and Wagnall's Standard Dictionary of Folklore, Mythology and Legend*, ed. Maria Leach; "The Making of the Races" is popular in East Africa and it is recounted by Jane Kurtz in *Ethiopia, the Roof of Africa*; the Kalenjin folktale is adapted from the version recounted by C. Chesaina in *Oral Literature of the Kalenjin*; "The Hare and the Lioness" is from *Whole World Book of Citations*; "The Iron Man" is adapted from the version published in *Opportunity* magazine, December 1923.

Bushman prisoner's statement is from Laurens Van der Post's novel *A Story Like the Wind*.

Dagara initiation ceremony song is from *Of Water and the Spirit* by Malidoma Patrice Somé.

Swahili superstitions are from *Swahili Sayings* by S. S. Farsi.

Egyptian expressions are from *Arabic Proverbs* by John Lewis Burckhardt.

Quotation from South African journalist Hettie V. was found in *Lives of Courage* by Diana Russell.

Yoruba proverbs are from *Yoruba Proverbs* by Raphael Odekunle, *Yoruba Proverbs: Translation and Annotation* by Oyekan Owomoyela and Bernth Lindfors; *A Ki: Yoruba Proscriptive and Prescriptive Proverbs,* and *Agbeka Oro Yoruba: Appropriate Words and Expressions in Yoruba* by Chief Isaac O. Delano.

Bini of Benin beliefs are from *At the Back of the Black Man's Mind* by R. E. Dennett.

Shona proverbs are from *Tsumo-Shumo: Shona Proverbial Lore and Wisdom* by Mordikai A. Hamutyinei and Albert B. Plangger.

Oromo proverbs are from *Proverbs and Sayings of the Oromo People of Ethiopia and Kenya* by George Cotter.

Nyanja of Malawi proverbs are from Ernest Gray's article "Some Proverbs of the Nyanja People."

Vai proverbs and folktales are from *Negro Culture in West Africa* by George W. Ellis.

Hausa folktales are from *Hausa Literature and the Hausa Sound System* by R. C. Abraham.

Soldiers' songs are from Anthony Clayton's paper *Communication for New Loyalties.*

Excerpt from "Song for Luanda" by Luandino Vieira is from *Poems From Angola,* ed. and trans. Michael Wolfers.

"Fortitude," anonymous Somali poem, is from *The Languages of the World* by Kenneth Katzner.

"The Oba of Benin"; description of the Ghanaian king's audiences; passage from Queen of Sheba's *Kebra Negast;* anonymous inscription at the city of Brass; traditional Akan poem; and El Mehmendar's description of Mansa Musa's visit to Egypt are all from *African Achievements* by Lester Brooks.

The African national anthem is in *The Rainbow People of God* by Desmond Tutu.

The full text of Grace Birabwa Isharaza's poem "Candlelight" can be found in *Summer Fires: New Poetry of Africa,* ed. Argus Calder and others.

The full text of Léopold Sédar Senghor's "Black Woman" can be found in *Selected Poems of Léopold Sédar Senghor,* comp. John Reed and Clive Wake.

Anonymous Somali poem beginning 'My brother is there...' is quoted by John Darnton in "A Barren Ethiopian Desert Is Promised Land to Somalis," *New York Times,* September 14, 1978.

"The Bench" by Richard Rive is from *The Penguin Book of Southern African Stories*, ed. Stephen Gray.

The Yoruba maxims beginning "Let us not run the world hastily..." (trans. E.B. Idowu) are from *The African Genius*, by Basil Davidson, p. 107.

Excerpt from "The Mystic Drum" by Gabriel Okara is from *Black Kingdoms Black Peoples* by Anthony Atmore and Gillian Stacey; originally from *Modern Poetry From Africa*, ed. Gerald Moore and Uli Beier.

Excerpt from Bernard Dadié's "I Thank You God" is from *Traveller's Literary Companion: Africa* by Oona Strathern; originally from *Voices From Twentieth Century Africa*, ed. Chinweizu. This poem can also be found in *The Negritude Poets*, ed. Ellen Conroy Kennedy.

The Bergdama of Namibia chant is from *Traveller's Literary Company: Africa* by Oona Strathern.

The predictions of Mbogo wa Kirangi and Embu songs are from *Embu Historical Texts* by H. S. K. Mwaniki, pp. 56, 65, 197.

Kalenjin of Kenya songs are from *Oral Literature of the Kalenjin* by C. Chesaina.

The "Song of the Turtle" is from *Ants Will Not Eat Your Fingers*, ed. Leonard Doob.

Excerpt from Chief Lobengula's letter to Queen Victoria is from *Inside Africa* by John Gunther, p. 602.

Excerpt from Ken Saro-Wiwa's "Africa Kills Her Sun" is from *African Rhapsody* by Nadezda Obradovic, pp. 296–97.

The main reference source for public holidays was the *Europa World Year Book 1995;* attempts were also made to confirm these dates with embassies.

Bibliography

Aardema, Verna. *Ji-Nongo-Nongo Means Riddles*, Four Winds Press, New York, 1978.

Abraham, R.C. *Hausa Literature and the Hausa Sound System*, University of London Press, 1959.

Amadi, Elechi. *Estrangement*, Heinemann, London, 1986.

Amoah, Osei, ed. *A Political Dictionary of Black Quotations*, Oyokoany-inaase House, London, 1989.

Atmore, Anthony, and Gillian Stacey. *Black Kingdoms Black Peoples*, G. P. Putnam's Sons, New York, 1979.

Baker, Daniel B., ed. *Political Quotations*, Gale Research, Detroit, 1990.

Barrett, Anthony J. *Turkana Way of Life*, N.p., Nairobi, 1988.

Beti, Mongo. *King Lazarus*, Heinemann, London, 1960.

Brooks, Lester. *African Achievements*, De Gustibus Press, 1992.

_____. *Great Civilizations of Ancient Africa*, Four Winds Press, New York, 1971.

Burckhardt, John Lewis. *Arabic Proverbs of the Modern Egyptians*, Curzon Press, London, 1984.

Calder, Argus, and others, eds. *Summer Fires: New Poetry of Africa*, Heinemann, Oxford, 1983.

Cheney-Coker, Syl. *The Last Harmattan of Alusine Dunbar*, Heinemann, London, 1990.

Chesaina, C. *Oral Literature of the Kalenjin*, Heinemann, Kenya, Nairobi, 1991.

Chinweizu, ed. *Voices From Twentieth Century Africa*, Faber and Faber, London, 1988.

Chraibi, Driss. *Heirs to the Past*, Heinemann, Oxford, 1971.

Clayton, Anthony. *Communication for New Loyalties: African Soldiers' Songs*, Center for International Studies, Ohio University, 1978.

Cotter, George. *Proverbs and Sayings of the Oromo People of Ethiopia and Kenya*, Edwin Mellen Press, Lewiston, N.Y., 1992.

Darnton, John. "A Barren Ethiopian Desert Is Promised Land to Somalis." *New York Times*, September 14, 1978.

Davidson, Basil. *The African Genius*, Little, Brown, Boston, 1969

Delano, Chief Isaac O. *Agbeka Oro Yoruba: Appropriate Words and Expressions in Yoruba*, Oxford University Press, London, 1960.

Deng, Francis Mading. *The Dinka of the Sudan*, Waveland Press, Ill., 1972.

Dennett, R.E. *At the Back of the Black Man's Mind*, Macmillan, New York, 1906.

Dodge, Cole P., and Magne Raundalen, eds. *War, Violence, and Children in Uganda*, Norwegian University Press, Oslo, 1987.

Doob, Leonard, ed. *Ants Will Not Eat Your Fingers*, Walker, New York, 1966.

Ellis, George W. *Negro Culture in West Africa*, Neale, New York, 1914.

Europa World Year Book 1995, Europa, London, 1995.

Evans, Humphrey. *The Mystery of the Pyramids*, Thomas Y. Crowell, New York, 1979.

Farsi, S. S. *Swahili Sayings*, Eastern Africa Publications, Dar Es Salaam, 1958.

Gray, Ernest. "Some Proverbs of the Nyanja People," *African Studies* 3, no. 3 (September 1944): 101.

Gray, Stephen, ed. *The Penguin Book of Southern Africa Stories*, New York, Penguin, 1985.

Gunther, John. *Inside Africa*, Harper and Brothers, New York, 1955.

Hamutyinei, Mordikai A., and Albert B. Plangger. *Tsumo-Shumo: Shona Proverbial Lore and Wisdom*, Mambo Press, Zimbabwe, 1987.

Kane, Cheikh Hamidou. *Ambiguous Adventure*, Heinemann, London, 1962.

Karodia, Farida. *A Shattering of Silence*, Heinemann, Oxford, 1993.

Katzner, Kenneth. *The Languages of the World*. New York: Funk & Wagnalls, 1975.

Kennedy, Ellen Conroy, ed. *The Negritude Poets*, Thunder's Mouth Press, New York, 1989.

King, Anita. *Quotes in Black*, Greenwood Press, London, 1981.

Knappert, Jan, ed. and trans. *A Choice of Flowers: Chaguo La Maua, An Anthology of Swahili Love Poetry*, Heinemann, London, 1972.

Kourouma, Ahmadou. *The Suns of Independence*, Heinemann, London, 1968.

Kunene Mazisi. *Zulu Poems*, Africana Publishing Corp., New York, 1970.

Kurtz, Jane. *Ethiopia, The Roof of Africa*, Dillon Press, New York, 1991.

Leach, Maria. ed. *Funk and Wagnall's Standard Dictionary of Folklore, Mythology and Legend*, Funk and Wagnall, New York, 1950.

Lentz, Harris M. III. *Heads of States and Governments*, McFarland, Jefferson, N.C., 1994.

Lindfors, Bernth, and Oyekan Owomoyela. *Yoruba Proverbs: Translation and Annotation*, Ohio University Center for International Studies, Athens, Ohio, 1973.

Lynch, Hollis. *Black Africa*, New York Times, 1973.

McCoy, Raymond A. *Ancient Egyptian Proverbs: Selections From the Instructions, Admonitions, and Exhortations of Wise Men and Teachers (2500–1000 B.C.)*, Stout State University, Menomonie, Wisconsin, 1971.

————. *The Golden Goddess: Ancient Egyptian Love Lyrics*, Enchiridion, Menomonie. Wis., 1972.

MacDonald, Margaret Read, ed. *The Folklore of World Holidays*, Gale Research, Detroit, 1992.

Madu, Raphael Okechukwu. *African Symbols, Proverbs and Myths, The Hermeneutics of Destiny*, Peter Lang, New York, 1992.

Mapanje, Jack, and Landeg White, eds. *Oral Poetry From Africa, An Anthology*, Longman Group, U.K., 1983.

M'Imanyara, Alfred M. *The Restatement of Bantu Origin and Meru History*, Longman Kenya, Nairobi, 1992.

Moore, George, and Uli Beier, eds. *Modern Poetry From Africa*, Penguin, Baltimore, 1963.

Mwangi, Rose. *Kikuyu Folktales, Their Nature and Value*, Kenya Literature Bureau, Nairobi, 1970.

Mwaniki, H. S. K. *Embu Historical Texts*, East Africa Literature Bureau, Nairobi, 1974.

————. *The Living History of Embu and Mbeere*, Kenya Literature Bureau, Nairobi, 1973.

Nyerere, Julius K. *Man and Development: Binadamu Na Maendeleo*, Oxford University Press, New York, 1974.

Obradovic, Nadezda. *African Rhapsody: Short Stories of the Contemporary African Experience*, Anchor, New York, 1994.

————. *Looking for a Rain God, An Anthology of Contemporary African Short Stories*, Simon and Schuster, New York, 1990.

Odekunle, Raphael. *Yoruba Proverbs*, Areje, Daystar, Ibadan, Nigeria, 1985.

Okara, Gabriel. *The Voice*, Africana, New York, 1970.

Owomoyela, Oyekan. *A Ki i: Yoruba Proscriptive and Prescriptive Proverbs*, University Press of America, Lanham, Md., 1988.

Ransley, John. *Chambers Dictionary of Political Biography*, W & R Chambers, Edinburgh, 1991.

Ruete, Emily. *Memoirs of an Arabian Princess From Zanzibar*, Marcus Wiener, New York, 1989.

Russell, Diana E. H. *Lives of Courage, Women for a New South Africa*, Basic Books, New York, 1989.

Schipper, Mineke. *Source of All Evil, African Proverbs and Sayings on Women*, Phoenix, Nairobi, 1991.

Searle, Chris. *We're Building a New School, Diary of a Teacher in Mozambique*, Zed Press, London, 1981.

Senghor, Léopold Sédar. *Selected Poems of Léopold Sédar Senghar.* Compiled by John Reed and Clive Wake, Antheneum, New York,

Somé, Malidoma Patrice. *Of Water and the Spirit*, G. P. Putnam's Sons, New York, 1994.

Steiner, Christopher B. *African Art in Transit*, Cambridge University Press, 1994.

Strathern, Oona. *Traveller's Literary Companion: Africa*, Passport, Lincolnwood, Ill., 1995.

Strouhal, Eugen. *Life of the Ancient Egyptians*, University of Oklahoma Press, Norman, 1992.

Tutu, Desmond. *The Rainbow People of God*. Edited by John Allen: Doubleday, New York, 1994.

Van der Post, Laurens. *A Story Like the Wind*, Hogarth Press, London, 1972.

Waters, M. W. *Cameos From the Kraal*, Juta, Johannesburg, c. 1900.

Webster, John ed. *Hope and Suffering: Desmond Tutu*. Grand Rapids, Mich.: William B. Eerdmans Publishing Co., 1984.

Westermarck, Edward. *Wit and Widsom in Morocco*, George Rutledge and Sons, London, 1930.

Patras, Kathryn and Ross, eds. *Whole World Book of Quotations*, Addison-Wesley, Reading, MA, 1995.

Wolfers, Michael, ed. and trans. *Peom From Angola*, Heinemann Educational Books, Exeter, N.H., 1979.

Yetiv, Isaac. *1,001 Proverbs from Tunisia*, Three Continents Press, Washington, D.C., 1987.

Indexes

HOLIDAYS BY COUNTRY

Note: Religious holidays are observed by Muslim and Christian communities throughout Africa. Major religious observations are not listed below by country; instead they appear on the approximate date on which they occur.

Algeria
> Anniversary of the Overthrow of Ben Bella, June 19
> Independence Day, July 5
> Anniversary of the Revolution, November 1

Angola
> Commencement of the Armed Struggle (against Portuguese colonialism), February 4
> Victory Day, March 27
> National Heroes' Day, (birthday of Dr. Agostinho Neto), September 17
> Independence Day, November 11
> Family Day, December 25

Benin
> National Day, August 1

Botswana
> President's Day, July 15–16
> Botswana Day, September 30–October 1

Burkina Faso
> Revolution Day (anniversary of the 1966 coup), January 3
> National Day, August 4
> Anniversary of the 1987 Coup, October 15
> Proclamation of the Republic, December 11

Burundi
> Independence Day, July 1
> Victory of Union for National Progress UPRONA (UPRONA) Party, September 18

174

Cameroon
Mount Cameroon Race, last Sunday of January (see Jan. 25)
Youth Day, February 11
National Day, May 20
Cape Verde
National Heroes' Day (anniversary of the death of Amílcar Cabral), January 20
Independence Day, July 5
Central African Republic
Boganda Day (anniversary of the death of the first president), March 29
National Day of Prayer, June 30
Independence Day, August 13
National Day, December 1
Chad
Independence Day, August 11
Proclamation of the Republic, November 28
Comoros
Independence Day, July 6
Anniversary of President Abdallah's Assassination, November 27
Congo
Independence Day, August 15
Côte d'Ivoire
Independence Day, December 7
Djibouti
Independence Day, June 27
Egypt
Coptic Christmas, January 7
Mother's Day, March 21
Sham an-Nessim (Coptic Easter), date varies (see April 17)
Sinai Liberation Day, April 25
Revolution Day, July 23
Armed Forces Day, October 6
Equatorial Guinea
Independence Day, March 5
Human Rights Day, December 10
Eritrea
Coptic Christmas, January 7
Timket (Eastern Orthodox Epiphany—baptism of Christ), January 19
Fasika (Easter Sunday), date varies (see May 7)
Independence Day, May 24
Martyrs' Day, June 20
Anniversary of the Start of the Armed Struggle, September 1
Maskal (Finding the True Cross), September 27

Liberia
Armed Forces Day, February 11
Decoration Day, March 12
J. J. Robert's Birthday (commemorates the birthday of the first president), March 15
Fast and Prayer Day, April 11
National Redemption Day (anniversary of the 1980 coup), April 12
National Unification Day, May 14
Independence Day, July 26
Flag Day, August 24
Thanksgiving Day, November 6
National Memorial Day, November 12
President Tubman's Birthday, November 29

Libya
Evacuation Day (commemorates the withdrawal of British troops at the end of World War II), March 28
Evacuation Day, June 11
Revolution Day, September 1
Evacuation Day, October 7

Madagascar
Memorial Day (commemorates the 1947 rebellion), March 29
Independence Day, June 26
Republic Day, December 30

Malawi
John Chilembwe Day (commemorates the freedom fighter's struggle against British colonial rule), January 16
Martyrs' Day, March 3
Freedom Day, June 14
Republic Day, July 6
Mother's Day, second Monday in October (see October 9)
National Tree Planting Day, December 21

Mali
Army Day, January 20
Independence Day, September 22
Anniversary of the 1968 Coup, November 19

Mauritania
National Day, November 28

Mauritius
Thaipoosam Cavadee (Tamil religious observance), February 4
Maha Shivratree (Hindu festival), February 17
Chinese Spring Festival, date varies (see February 19)
National Day, March 12

Sierra Leone
  Independence Day, April 27
Somalia
  Independence Day, June 26
  Foundation of the Republic, July 1
South Africa
  Human Rights Day, March 21
  Family Day, March 31
  Founders' Day (founding of Cape Town), April 6
  Freedom Day, April 27
  Youth Day, June 16
  National Women's Day, August 9
  Heritage Day, September 24
  Kruger Day (commemorates Paul Kruger, the president of the South
    African Republic (1883–89), October 10
  Day of Reconciliation, December 16
  Day of Goodwill, December 26
Sudan
  Independence Day, January 1
  Coptic Christmas, January 7
  National Unity Day, March 3
  Uprising Day (anniversary of the 1985 coup), April 6
  Sham an-Nassim (Coptic Easter Monday), date varies (see April 17)
  Revolution Day, June 30
  Decentralization Day, July 1
Swaziland
  Commonwealth Day, date varies, (see March 11)
  King's Birthday (Mswati III), April 19
  National Flag Day, April 25
  King's Birthday (Sobhuza II), July 22
  Umhlanga (Reed Dance Day), August 24
  Somhlolo (Independence Day), September 6
  United Nations Day, October 24
Tanzania
  Zanzibar Revolution Day, January 12
  Youth Day, February 5
  Union Day (National Day), April 26
  Saba Saba (International Trade Fair Day), July 7
  Nane Nane (Farmers' Day), August 8
  Independence Day, December 9
Togo
  Liberation Day (anniversary of the 1967 coup), January 13
  Day of Victory (anniversary of failed attack at Sarakawa), January 24

COUNTRIES AND ETHNIC GROUPS

Akan, January 10, February 29, March 23, November 30

Algeria, June 19, July 5, August 28, November 1

Angola, February 4, March 27, April 14, September 17, November 11, December 25

Ashanti, March 9, April 28

Bakongo, October 14

Bambara, September 22, November 22

Baule, June 20

Benin, August 1

Berber, November 28

Bergdama, May 16

Bini, April 1, July 19

Botswana, July 15, September 30

Burkina Faso, January 3, August 4, October 15, December 11

Burundi, July 1, September 18

Cameroon, January 25, February 11, May 20, July 28, August 12, September 29, November 11

Cape Verde, January 20, July 5

Central African Republic, March 29, June 30, August 13, December 1

Chad, November 28, December 1

Comoros, July 6, November 27

Congo, February 13, 26, August 15

Côte d'Ivoire, February 3, 20, March 24, June 20, 29, July 3, 11, October 29, December 7, 23, 26

Dagara, August 23

Dinka, August 29

Djibouti, June 27

Egypt, January 1, 7, 14, 15, February 14, 16, 17, 22, 28, March 10, 18, 21, 22, 31, April 8, 17, 21, 25, May 5, 8, 19, June 12, 15, 21, July 17, 21, 23, 29, 31, August 19, September 4, 15, 16, October 6, 16, 19, 28, 31, November 15, 20, December 6, 14, 20, 31

Embu, January 31, March 4, September 1, October 3

Equatorial Guinea, March 5, December 10

Eritrea, January 7, 19, May 7, 24, June 20, September 1, 27

Morocco, January 23, March 3, 22, May 17, 23, June 17, July 9, August 14, 20, September 26, October 5, November 1, 6, 13, 18, December 17

Mozambique, February 3, April 7, May 2, June 25, September 7, 25

Namibia, March 21, May 4, 16, August 15, December 10

Ndebele, June 11

Niger, April 15, August 3, December 18

Nigeria, January 21, 24, 28, February 2, 15, March 7, 13, April 1, 16, May 12, June 10, 18, July 13, 18, 20, August 5, 6, 25, September 2, 8, 10, 13, 19, October 1, 8, 17, 25, 30, November 5, 9, 16, 23, December 2, 13, 27

Nyanja, January 16, March 19, May 6, June 2, 14, September 20, October 22

Oromo, March 25, April 23, May 26, July 4, 27, September 27

Ovimbundu, March 27

Rwanda, July 1, September 25, October 26

São Tomé and Príncipe, July 12

Senegal, February 8, 21, April 4, 10, May 1, 15, July 14, August 10, December 21

Seychelles, June 5, 29, December 8

Sierra Leone, April 27, May 11, June 7, October 9

Shona, January 27, April 18, August 11

Somalia, January 29, June 13, 26, 27, July 1, 2, August 22, November 3, December 19, 29

Songhai, December 18

South Africa, January 8, 22, February 1, 11, March 21, 31, April 5, 6, 19, 27, May 9, 25, 31, June 16, 26, July 15, 16, 22, August 2, 9, 26, September 6, 24, October 4, 7, 10, November 10, December 4, 5, 16, 26

Sudan, January 1, 7, March 3, April 13, 17, May 29, June 30, July 1, August 16, 29, September 21, December 24

Swahili, January 12, 17, 30, February 25, March 16, 30, April 30, May 27, June 5, 6, 22, 28, July 8, 30, August 30, September 14, 23, October 21, November 2, 25, December 8, 28

Swaziland, March 11, April 19, 25, July 22, August 24, September 6, October 24

Tanzania, Jaunary 12, February 1, 5, April 26, 29, July 7, August 8, 21, September 1, December 9

Togo, January 13, 24, April 24, 27, September 24

Tunisia, January 18, February 14, March 20, 21, April 9, 24, May 10, June 4, July 25, August 13, September 3, 9, October 15, November 7, December 3

Turkana, October 11

Twi, November 17, December 10

Uganda, January 26, June 3, 9, July 10, October 9, November 21

Vai, February 9, March 12, April 11, 12, August 24, September 5, November 12

SPEAKER

Achebe, Chinua (1930–); Nigerian, one of Africa's most widely read novelists: April 16, September 10

Akello, Grace; Ugandan poet: January 26

Akhenaten; ancient Egyptian king: June 21

Al Bekri; Moorish historian: February 12

Amadi, Elechi; Nigerian writer: November 5

Augustine, Saint (A.D. 354–430); Catholic saint from Tagaste, North Africa, his feast day is August 28: August 28

Azikiwe, Nnamdi; first president of Nigeria (1963–1966): October 1

Banda, Hastings Kamuzu (1906–); first president of Malawi (1966–): July 6

Bedri, Babikr (1861–1954); Sudanese scholar: August 16

Bemba, Sylvain; Congolese writer: February 26

Ben Bella, Ahmed; first president of Algeria: June 19

Ben Jelloun, Tahar; Moroccan novelist and poet: November 1

Beti, Mongo; Cameroonian novelist: May 20, July 28, August 12, September 29

Biko, Steve (1946–1977); South African political activist, died while in police custody: March 21, May 25, July 16

Cavafy, C. P. (1863–1933); native of Alexandria, Egypt, became renowned during his lifetime as a great figure of modern Greek poetry: March 18

Cheney-Coker, Syl; Sierra Leonean writer: May 11

Chinodya, Shimmer; Zimbabwean writer: May 3

Chraibi, Driss; Moroccan writer: May 17, August 14, September 26

Cogoano, Ottobah (eighteenth century); antislavery activist originally from Ghana: February 10

Dadié, Bernard; Ivorian writer: December 26

De Silveria, Elisa; Mozambican schoolgirl: September 7

Diescho, Joseph; Namibian novelist: August 15

Diop, David Mandessi (1927–1960); Senegalese poet: February 21

Diori, Hamani (1906–1989); first president of Niger (1960–1974): August 3

Duauf; ancient Egyptain magistrate: September 4

El Mehmendar (fourteenth-century); Egyptian emir: February 22

Enahoro, Anthony; Nigerian writer: October 1

Equiano, Oldanah (eighteenth-century); West African writer: December 1

Mboya, Tom (1930–1969); Kenyan labor and nationalist leader, assassinated in Nairobi: June 1

Memmi, Albert; Tunisian novelist and poet: September 3

Menelik II (1844–1913); emperor of Ethiopia (1889–1913): March 2, December 25

Müller, Piet; South African journalist: April 6

Neferhotep; high priest of Amon in ancient Egypt: February 16

Neto, Agostinho (1922–1979); first president of Angola (1975–1979): September 17

Nkrumah, Kwame (1909–1972); first president of Ghana (1957–1966): March 6, 8

Nuur, Faarah; Somali clan leader and poet: June 27

Nyerere, Julius Kambarage (1922–   ); first president of Tanzania (1962–1985), also known as a philosopher and translator of Shakespeare into Kiswhaili: February 1, 5, April 26, July 7, August 8, 21, December 9

Okara, Gabriel; Nigerian writer: July 20, August 5, October 30, December 2

Okoye, Mowugo; Nigerian writer: January 28

Paton, Alan Stewart (1903–1988); South African writer, "called the conscience of white South Africa": April 27, August 26

Peters, Lenrie; poet from the Gambia: February 18

Rabearivelo, Jean-Joseph (1901–1937); Malagasy poet: December 30

Rive, Richard; South African writer: October 4

Roberts, Shabaan (1909–1962); Swahili poet: September 14

Ruete, Emily; Arabian princess from Zanzibar: April 29

Sadat, Anwar el- (1918–1981); Egyptian president (1970–1981), Nobel peace price recipient (1978), along with Israeli prime minister Menachem Begin: April 25, May 5

Said, Laila; Egyptian playwright, director, and teacher: January 1

Salih, Tayeb; Sudanese writer: September 21, December 24

Samatar, Said Sheikh; Somali scholar: January 29

Saro-Wiwa, Ken (1941–1995); Nigerian writer: June 18

Senghor, Léopold Sédar; first president of Senegal (1960–1980) and poet: February 8, April 4, May 15, July 14, August 10

Sese Seko, Mobutu (1930–   ); president of Zaire (1965–   ): October 27

Sheba, (c. tenth-century B.C.); Ethiopian queen: February 24

Soglo, Nicéphore; president of Benin (1991–1996): August 1

Taha, Mahmoud Mohammed (1909–1985); Sudanese reformer: May 29

Terence (c. 190–59 B.C.); comic-poet of ancient Rome, originally from North Africa: February 14

Thiong'o, Ngugi wa; Kenyan writer: May 13

Touré, Ahmed Sékou (1922–1984); first president of Guinea (1958–1984): February 6, August 27, October 2

SUBJECT

abundance, Dec. 1
adaptability, Feb. 26
accounts, Sept. 9
advice, May 8, Nov. 13
Africa, Jan. 3, 26, Feb. 5, 19, 21, March 6, April 16, 19, June 9, Sept. 17, Nov. 24, 29
African National Anthem, Feb. 7
age, June 16, 20, 24, July 22, Sept. 27, Dec. 27
agreement, June 13, Aug. 31
America, Feb. 3, June 26
ancestors, Jan. 3, Feb. 8
anger, July 23, Nov. 16
anonymity, Aug. 24
Arabs, April 25
arrogance, June 8, Nov. 6, 8, 9
articulateness, July 9
bad deeds, May 4
baobab trees, Oct. 18
beauty, Jan. 5, Sept. 10, Nov. 8, 9
black pride, Feb. 21, July 16, Aug. 10, Dec. 26
boastfulness, June 14, Aug. 6, 18, Sept. 5, Oct. 13, 19
bowls, Feb. 4
bravery, Sept. 1
brother, Sept. 9
business, Sept. 9
Cape Town, April 6
Cape Verde Islands (creation of), Jan. 20
capitalism, Feb. 3
catalysts, Aug. 22
Catholicism, Aug. 15
change, Aug. 20, Nov. 18
character, March 26, July 26, Sept. 14, Oct. 25

charity, Feb. 16, July 21
cheap, Jan. 13
cheating, June 12
children, June 22, Nov. 10
Christians, Dec. 25
Christmas, Jan. 7
cities, March 18, Sept. 3, Nov. 11
civilization, May 15, June 26, Sept. 29
cleverness, Jan. 6, Sept. 5
clingy person, Jan. 15
colonialism, April 18, May 22, June 26, 30, Sept. 7, Oct. 27, Dec. 25
commoners, Oct. 1
compatability, Aug. 31
compensation, Nov. 12
comprehension, Dec. 20
conclusions, Nov. 4
confidence, Jan. 11, Sept. 24
conformity, March 19, July 15, 20, Sept. 30, Nov. 4
contentedness, June 7, Oct. 15
corruption, June 18
courage, April 2
criticism, May 8
cruelty, Sept. 17
culture, Jan. 3, Feb. 6, 19, April 4, July 6
customs, May 21
dancing, Oct. 30
danger, Dec. 6
death, Jan. 31, Feb. 28, Oct. 28
destiny, March 20
dignity, Feb. 1, Sept. 29, Oct. 2
discretion, May 26
discrimination, July 7
divisiveness, Aug. 17
divorce, March 25
dogs, Jan. 8

More Books of African-American Interest

Carol Publishing Group proudly publishes dozens of books of African-American interest. From history to contemporary issues facing Black Americans and popular culture, these books take a compelling look at the African-American experience.

The African-American Book of Days
by Julia Stewart
A daily account of key events in African-American history.
$16.95 paper 0-8065-1661-5

The African-American Health Book
by Valiere Alcena
Educates about diseases and their treatments, especially those that significantly afflict the black population.
$12.95 paper 0-8065-1719-0

The African-American Heritage Cookbook
by Carolyn Quick Tillery
Captures not only the traditional tastes, but also the emotions of Tuskegee, the historic black university founded by Booker T. Washington.
$18.95 cloth 1-55972-325-4

The African Cookbook
by Bea Sandler
Authentic recipes from all over the continent of Africa that can be prepared using easily obtainable ingredients.
$12.95 paper 0-8065-1398-5

African Proverbs & Wisdom
by Julia Stewart
Essential both as a historical calendar and as a highly browsable commemoration of African culture—culled from 25 African nations.
$12.95 paper 0-8065-1807-3

The Black 100
by Columbus Salley
A unique history book that not only selects the most significant African-Americans ever, but ranks them according to their contributions in the struggle for equality.
$18.95 paper 0-8065-1550-3

A Complete History of the Negro Leagues, 1884-1955 by Mark Ribowsky
The first exhaustive history of the Negro Leagues ever written. As much a social commentary as it is a sports book.
$18.95 paper 0-8065-1868-5

Denzel Washington: His Films & Career
by Douglas Brode
Takes readers onto the sets of his films and behind the scenes to reveal the best of a preeminent talent.
$22.50 cloth 1-55972-381-5

The Healthy Soul Food Cookbook
by Wilbert Jones
Takes a second look at traditional African-American cuisine and shares contemporary healthier versions.
$12.95 paper 0-8065-1863-4

First Lady of Song: Ella Fitzgerald for the Record by Geoffrey Mark Fidelman
The life story of the legendary lady of jazz—a celebration of Ella's life and work.
$17.95 paper 0-8065-1771-9

1,001 African Names by Julia Stewart
Names for adults to name their children or for anyone to substitute for their own names—arranged alphabetically along with their English translations.
$10.95 paper 0-8065-1737-9

Revelations: The Autobiography of Alvin Ailey
The poignant life story of the pioneering choreographer.
$14.95 paper 0-8065-1861-8

Ask for these African-American Interest books at your bookstore. To place an order, or for a free descriptive brochure, call 1-800-447-BOOK or send your name and address to Carol Publishing Group, 120 Enterprise Ave., Dept. 51807, Secaucus, NJ 07094.